The
Innovative
ADMIN

Unleash the Power of Innovation In Your Administrative Career

By

JULIE PERRINE

CAP-OM, MBTI Certified

Founder of All Things Admin
A Julie Perrine International, LLC Company

www.AllThingsAdmin.com
www.TheInnovativeAdmin.com

ISBN: 0982943016
ISBN 978-0-9829430-1-4
Printed in the United States of America
10 9 8 7 6 5 4 3 2 1
First Paperback Edition

Dedication

In Memory of Kathy Fisher —
One of the most innovative admins
I've ever had the opportunity to work with.
Your inspiration lives on!

Table of Contents

Foreword

Administrative professionals play key roles in every industry. They work in both generalized and specialized positions, at entry level and with graduate degrees. Support professionals are often the glue, the hub, the gatekeeper, the calm eye in the center of the storm of corporate activity. The challenge is there is no clear definition, no reliable measure, and no consensus on what makes an excellent administrative professional. In *The Innovative Admin*, Julie Perrine has hit on a key factor in what makes one admin rise above the others. That factor is innovation.

Early in my career, I had an assistant named Penny. Penny didn't just do her job, she helped me do mine better. If I needed a certain document, she knew where it was and had it copied, collated, and placed on my desk before I even asked. She fielded questions from staff, board members and clients. They knew she knew what I didn't know or forgot I knew. Penny always made me look good – personally and professionally. She was an efficient colleague and trusted confidant. We were a team. Her best gift was her ability to bounce ideas around with me as we collaborated on new solutions for our clients. Penny was open to innovation. This made her priceless to me.

A few years later I had another assistant I'll call Sue. Sue prided herself on her efficiency. She had been providing support to executives for years and came with excellent references. It became clear early on that Sue was going to have a hard time excelling in this position. Sue was very traditional and most comfortable doing things the same way she had always done them. Our office was very diverse, made up of creative, out-of-the-box change-agents. Sue could type at the speed of lightning, take concise meeting minutes, and kept an exceptionally organized desk. But Sue was unable to see herself as part of a problem solving team. Sue lost her job, not because she did anything wrong, but because she didn't do anything better. Sue was not open to innovation.

Twenty-five years ago, an admin's primary responsibilities included transcribing, sending documents, and scheduling meetings. Technical innovations have resulted in software that handles those tasks for me now. But at this point in time, I work with several support professionals who handle everything from web design to event planning for my business. I rely on these professionals to know what I don't know and offer solutions I don't even know I need. The times demand professionals who are prepared to offer creative solutions and new ideas. The times demand professionals who are prepared to innovate.

There is no one better equipped to write *The Innovative Admin* than Julie Perrine. For over a decade I've watched her career catapult. Her accomplishments are due to her never-ending pursuit of personal and professional growth. Julie Perrine embodies *The Innovative Admin*. She challenges support professionals to see all the potential in themselves and their profession.

Innovation is the catalyst to growth. Research has shown that some of the best and most sustainable growth occurs from ideas generated at the most "hands-on" level of a workforce. The business culture that embraces creative thinking and change agency will be blessed with growth and profitability. The same is true for the administrative professionals that embrace innovative thinking.

You can choose to be a valued team-member and collaborator in your company. *The Innovative Admin* will chart the course.

~ Dr. Lisa Van Allen

Dr. Lisa Van Allen is the Biz Doctor. She helps entrepreneurs and executives identify the beliefs that are barriers to success and implement strategies that support a life of passion, purpose and profitability. Her book The Belief Quotient *is being published by Hay House/Balboa Publishers in spring 2012.*

Getting Started

Welcome to the next journey on your administrative career path that will lead you toward becoming *The Innovative Admin*. I'm so glad you're here.

Review the Roadmap and Chart Your Course

To get started using this book, read it through from cover to cover to gain a good overview of the components involved in becoming *The Innovative Admin*. As you read, flag or highlight the chapters where you know you need to spend more time later. Most of the chapters contain a plan of action at the end to give you a roadmap for getting started and taking immediate action. Once you have a good overview of all of the material, use this book as a guide to chart your course throughout the upcoming year. You may want to break it down into weekly or monthly goals so you stay on track. The best way to make changes and experience results is to take action and track your progress.

Your Implementation Plan

For your convenience, we have made all of the action plans from this book (plus a cover) available in an electronic download at **www.The-InnovativeAdmin.com**. We did this so you can download these action plans, put them in a three ring binder (your Innovation Binder!), and use them to begin tracking your personal progress and transformation over the coming weeks as you implement what you learn.

I also recommend you start a journal or insert blank sheets of lined paper in your Innovation Binder to begin journaling as you work through the material. You will want something in which to take notes and capture thoughts as you are inspired by the various examples and ideas shared throughout this book. Having your action plans and writing paper in the same binder will keep you organized.

My Writing Style

I tend to write in a more conversational style. While I do believe in good grammar, correct punctuation, and complete sentences, there may be places where I stray a bit for emphasis. But fear not, my proofing and editing team tries to keep me in line. I share this because I know how particular we admins can be. It is, after all, what we do for a living – proofing other people's documents. That said, if you find an error that we should correct in future editions, please visit the Contact Us page at www.TheInnovativeAdmin.com and kindly let us know.

A lot of what I'm going to share and recommend requires you put some thought and effort into making changes in how you currently think and work. It will require establishing new habits and eliminating old habits that are not supporting you in this endeavor. There are no shortcuts. You have to do the inner work to experience the outer results of change and transformation you are looking for in your life and career.

At times, my approach is direct and to the point. But if you've heard me speak, participated in any of my training programs, or regularly follow my writing online, you'll know I always tackle issues with a positive, proactive, take-charge attitude. This book is no exception. *So if you're ready to transform your thoughts and behaviors—and in doing so, transform your career*—**let's get started!**

Part 1: Introduction

"Being willing to do what others will not, will always give you the competitive edge."

~Robin Crow

Chapter 1:

The Latest Innovation is You!

"Innovation distinguishes between a leader and a follower."

~ Steve Jobs

Take a look around any office and it's not hard to find the latest innovations in software, electronic devices, and furniture. But as innovative as those things may have been when they were first purchased, they quickly become obsolete because another idea inevitably follows, resulting in the latest and greatest thing everyone has to have.

The same thing can happen to us in our administrative careers. If we don't stay on top of our game and consistently engage in strategic activities to develop and advance our thinking, we'll become obsolete over time and risk replacement as well. Do you want to be an administrative professional who has skills that are in high demand? Do you want to command a top salary in your field? Do you want to be a leader in your profession? To avoid extinction, you must become *The Innovative Admin*.

Admins and entrepreneurs are the two audiences I have primarily supported throughout my career. Part of my personal mission has always been to connect them to the most innovative ideas, technologies, and people that I possibly can. If I don't have the solutions, I want to act as the conduit to find and provide the solutions. I never want someone to ask me a question I've been asked before and not have the answer. As I've applied this principle over the years, it has led me down trails I may never have discovered which has helped me create new mental pathways for future expansion. And they always expand. It's like stretching a rubber band. Over time, the rubber band cannot retract to its original size because it has been stretched for so long. Your mind and your innovative thinking skills are the same. The more you train yourself to think innovatively, the more it happens without you having to consciously think about doing it.

In an article entitled, "The Evolution of Duties," published by the International Association of Administrative Professionals (IAAP), they compare how the typical duties of the administrative profession have evolved over the past two decades.[1] The duties of decades past included handling clerical duties, supporting one manager, taking minutes at meetings, and being more of a low-level assistant. Today's administrative support role serves at a much higher level. You must be prepared to manage projects, lead process improvements, master integrated computer software applications, support multiple executives, and work as a partner, team player, and contributing part of the management team. These new expectations and job responsibilities require a more innovative approach to stay on top of the technology and advanced knowledge of key business functions.

Are you an innovator? Do you know how to become more innovative in your thinking? If you already are, then what else can you do to keep expanding your innovation skills? That's what we're about to explore together.

"Getting by" is no longer enough. You must lead the charge toward advancing your skills, thinking, and professional network if you want to remain relevant. As an administrative professional, it is absolutely vital to your long-term success that you continually pursue innovative people, ideas, and technology – that you continually reinvent and renew yourself – that you become *The Innovative Admin*.

Chapter 2:

What
is
Innovation?

*"Creativity is thinking up new things.
Innovation is doing new things."*

~ Ted Levitt

love innovation because it's a new way of thinking about and doing things. It's how we take common, ordinary things and make
them better. It's how we make ourselves better. The goal of innovation is positive change and improvement. Unfortunately, we
don't often allow time for innovative thinking or create the environment required to inspire a transformation. As success-minded
administrative professionals, we must!

Do you remember art class in elementary school? I do. Once
the teacher gave us assignments, I dove in immediately and began
drawing the picture, creating the clay pot, or building the three
dimensional object, instinctively using my imagination and all of
the creative skills I could muster. Creativity abounded. I was, after
all, a talented artist as were all of my classmates. If you wanted

proof, all you had to do was walk down the school hallways lined with our artwork or look at the oddly shaped clay vases proudly displayed in our mothers' kitchens. But as we got older, something changed. The limitless potential of our creative ideas somehow dissipated. We weren't as confident in our creative potential and many times suppressed it for fear of what others might say or think about it. As adults, we continue to downplay or stifle our creative potential which ultimately limits our ability to generate innovative ideas, too.

Dennis Stauffer, author of *Thinking Clockwise*, talks about this in his report, "*The four greatest ways we stop ourselves...in business and in life:*"

> In his book *Orbiting the Giant Hairball*, Gordon Mackenzie, who was once known as the "creative paradox" at Hallmark, tells how much he enjoyed visiting schools. He would typically set up in the gym and lead sessions with each grade level, beginning with the first graders and working up. When he spoke, he would note all the student art work he saw on the walls of the school and say how nice it was to be among so many other artists. Then he would ask how many artists were in the room. With the first graders, every hand would go up enthusiastically. By the second grade, about half went up, just shoulder height. By the sixth grade, only a few would sheepishly raise their hands, apparently fearing the judgment of their peers.
>
> That's what we've done to ourselves, and continue to do to our children—with the best of intentions. We've been conditioned to suppress our creative impulses and with them our capacity to innovate. When the world was stable and predictable, this may have been adaptive. When we could learn a trade or a profession and get a job for life, having a fixed skill set and a head full of ready answers was the path to success. But none of us lives in that world anymore. We

live in a much more dynamic place where we need to constantly learn and unlearn and relearn, where imagination and insight are now our path to success and fixed ideas are almost certain to be inadequate. The behaviors we've been taught to suppress are now exactly the ones we need most![2]

Read that last paragraph again and reflect a bit. Are you suppressing your creative impulses? Is your job and work environment stable and predictable? Have you been able to get by without learning any new skills in your job? What are you doing to stimulate your imagination and gain insight as an admin?

Innovation…More than Creative Thinking

Innovative ideas may begin with creative thinking, but innovation is more than just critical or creative thinking or brainstorming where you are coming up with new ideas. Innovation comes when you actually IMPLEMENT the ideas you generate. It's doing something different than how it's always been done while adding value to those affected by that action.

Another great resource on this topic, Smartstorming.com, defines the primary difference between creativity and innovation like this:

Creativity is most often defined as the mental ability to conceptualize (imagine) new, unusual, or unique ideas, to see the new connection between seemingly random or unrelated things.

Innovation on the other hand, is defined as the process that transforms those forward-looking new ideas into real world (commercial) products, services, or processes of enhanced value. The result of such a transformation can be incremental, evolutionary or radical in its impact on the status quo. In other words, it can represent a natural step forward in a concept's development, a leap to the next gen-

eration of that concept, or a completely new and different
way of doing something altogether.[3]

Creativity is the mental ability everyone has. Innovation is pro-
ducing action and results – in effect, implementation. Innovative
thinking requires a change in the thought process altogether. It's a
systematic rethink of how we plan, engage, and solve problems as
admins. It's the process we use to convert the creative ideas into
realized results. Creativity is important, but becoming an innovator doesn't stop with creative thinking alone.

David Magellan Horth, Senior Enterprise Associate at the
Center for Creative Leadership, explains it like this:

> Innovative thinking doesn't rely on past experiences or
> known facts. It imagines a desired future state and figures
> out how to get there. It is intuitive and open to possibility.
> Rather than identifying right answers or wrong answers,
> the goal is to find a better way and explore multiple pos-
> sibilities.[4]

You must be able to not only see that desired future state but be able
to map out your plan of attack to make it happen – implementation!

Why is Innovation Important?

As admins, we are always expected to be prepared, to be ready for
anything, to have the answers, or to know how to find the answers.
If you want to become more than just the secretary or administrative assistant, if you want to be recognized as an administrative
leader in your organization, you MUST become an innovator.

We didn't continue using manual typewriters when electric
typewriters were invented. We didn't keep using mimeograph ma-
chines when the photocopier came along. As administrative professionals, we cannot keep doing things the way they've always been

done if we want to remain relevant and in demand. The alternative is extinction…just like the manual typewriter. Sure, someone may come by and use you just for old time's sake, but they won't tap into you as a resource because they don't recognize you as cutting edge, value-added, and efficient. You will become irrelevant because you haven't put in the time and effort to remain in high demand.

The great news is that you can learn to become more innovative. As the economy continues to change and evolve, you don't need to be scared or afraid of what's next for you in your job and career. You can remain vibrant and successful **if** you commit to becoming *The Innovative Admin*.

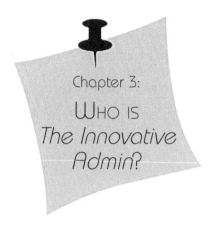

Chapter 3:

WHO IS
*The Innovative
Admin?*

*"The innovation point is the pivotal moment when talented
and motivated people seek the opportunity to act
on their ideas and dreams."*

~ W. Arthur Porter

efore we go any further, let's define *The Innovative Admin*. *The
Innovative Admin* is an administrative professional who intro-
duces, creates, or applies new or renewed ideas or methods
of doing things to the office environment. This is someone who
is actively doing, seeking, and implementing, not someone who
is simply coming up with ideas or maintaining the status quo. It's
more than simply generating creative ideas; it's the implementation of ideas that add value for your team members and customers.

By continually exposing yourself to innovative people, ideas,
and technology, you will begin to see where you can apply these
things to what you do each and every day for those you support.
Those you support will begin to view you as a forward-thinking,

cutting-edge, value-added, innovative professional who provides not only new perspectives on how to accomplish things, but also demonstrates the willingness to lead the charge in applying those new ideas and methods to the work you do.

My purpose with this book is to:

- Help you discover the simple things you can do to expose yourself to inspiring people, ideas, and technology on a regular basis;

- Give you step-by-step, action-oriented plans to help you become more innovative;

- Empower you to implement your innovative ideas each day as an administrative professional; and

- Help you to become more confident, prepared, and inspired to take charge of your career.

As I've applied the strategies I share throughout this book to my own career, I've experienced extraordinary personal and professional growth. My network has expanded in unbelievable ways. I've had the privilege of working with and learning from some amazing people. I've been presented with opportunities I never imagined. And I have turned an entry-level, receptionist job into a career of administrative support that has taken me from a supporting role in the executive office to becoming the CEO of my own company. I have a career that I absolutely love! This didn't happen overnight. It has taken years to develop my skills, to build upon and learn from my experiences, and to expand my innovative capacity. But the results have been worth every ounce of time and energy I have invested!

Your career path and desired outcomes may differ from mine, but the things you must pursue to achieve career advancement and fulfillment are still the same. Whether you feel like your career is stuck in a rut or you simply want to explore additional ways to keep your career positively moving forward, you'll find support here. It's never too late to start! You *can* create the career you've always imagined.

It's time to unleash the power of innovation in your administrative career and become known as ***The Innovative Admin***!

PART 2: THE FOUNDATIONAL COMPONENTS OF BECOMING *The Innovative Admin*

When you build a house, you begin by laying the foundation so you have a solid, stable base to support the structure itself. This same analogy applies to becoming *The Innovative Admin*. Before we look at some of the specific strategies you should apply to develop and expand your innovation potential, we need to explore the foundational components of innovative thinking that create the solid, stable base you must have in place first. Those are:

- Choose the Innovation Mindset

- Understand How the Innovation Mindset Works

- Turn Your Thinking Upside Down

- Collaborate to Innovate

- Know Yourself Inside Out

"To get what we've never had, we must do what we've never done."

~ Anonymous

Chapter 4

Choose the Innovation Mindset

"You can create an extraordinary career by changing your mindset."

~ Fabienne Fredrickson

O ne of the first things you must to do to become more innovative is choose the innovation mindset.

Mindset is the characteristic mental attitude that determines how you will interpret and respond to situations. Mindsets are powerful beliefs you hold. Your mindset is what influences how you think and how you act; it's your personal operating system. Thoughts create feelings and beliefs which lead to the actions you take and the results you see and experience. Sometimes the feelings and beliefs you have were passed on to you by others (family, friends, colleagues, media) or resulted from bad experiences you may have had. The key is to not let them sabotage your success moving forward. It's your responsibility to recognize and change them. You have to make the mental shift internally before you can expect to see different results externally.

In her book *Mindset*, Dr. Carol Dweck identified two mindsets that prevail: the fixed mindset and the growth mindset.[5]

The **fixed mindset** believes that your intelligence is static, your qualities are carved in stone, and it creates an urgency for you to prove yourself over and over. The fixed mindset leads to a desire to look smart and therefore a tendency to avoid challenges, get defensive and give up easily when obstacles appear, see effort as fruitless, ignore useful negative feedback, and feel threatened by the success of others. As a result, the person with this mindset may plateau early and achieve less than his or her full potential.

The **growth mindset**, however, believes the hand you're dealt is just the starting point for development. Intelligence can be developed which leads to a desire to learn and therefore a tendency to embrace challenges, persist in the face of obstacles, use effort as the path to mastery, learn from criticism, and find lessons and inspiration in the success of others. As a result, they reach ever-higher levels of achievement. It's based on the belief that your basic qualities are things you can cultivate through your efforts. Although people may differ in every way – in talents, personality, aptitudes, interests, temperaments – everyone can change and grow through application and experience.

I refer to these two mindsets as the **status quo (fixed) mindset** and **the innovation (growth) mindset**. For the purposes of discussing mindsets throughout this book, that's how I will refer to them.

If you want more than just momentary blips of innovation to permeate your thoughts, you have to identify what's holding you back and remove it. The first place to evaluate is your mindset. Do you have a status quo mindset or an innovation mindset?

Here are a few clues that may help you identify where you are on the mindset spectrum. I often hear comments like these from admins stuck in a status quo mindset:

- "I don't have to know that in my job. We have a department that handles it for us."

- "I would never use that in my current position."

- "Nothing in that training applied to me; I don't have to do that on my job."

- "We can't use Facebook or Twitter at work anyway. They have those sites blocked."

- "We hire an outside firm to do our website design work. I don't need those skills."

- "I'm planning to retire in just 'X' years, so that doesn't apply to me."

You will not be able to become more innovative without changing how you think about and do some things. You won't achieve your objectives if you aren't willing to remove the obstacles in your way. The status quo mindset will keep you firmly planted right where you currently are.

In contrast, these are comments I hear from admins who choose the innovation mindset:

- "I have never used that software before, but I'm very willing to learn it."

- "I have no idea how social media works, but I know my company is starting to use it, so I am attending webinars to get it figured out."

- "I am developing new skills to add to my résumé by volunteering on committees in professional associations."

- "I'd like to do more marketing and communications related work in my next job, so I've enrolled in some college courses to prepare me for that transition."

Admins who want to become more innovative must commit to the innovation mindset for the long term. This isn't a one-time activity; it's a life-long pursuit. It's about stretching yourself and becoming smarter. It's about seeking challenge and learning to thrive on it. It takes time for a seed to grow into a blooming flower. The innovation mindset gives you permission to realize you haven't learned everything yet, and that's okay. The innovation mindset embraces progress, not perfection.

Your mindset is a powerful thing! It can make or break you professionally. It can be the catalyst for amazing success or ultimate failure because your mindset ultimately controls your actions. But the good news is YOU can change your mindset. You have the power to choose which mindset you'll embrace, so choose the innovation mindset.

PLAN OF ACTION:

☐ Consciously choose the innovation mindset. Commit to taking positive, forward action daily – even if you only do one thing toward becoming a more innovative thinker each day.

☐ Think about and identify the obstacles (e.g., people, beliefs, etc.) that may be holding you back. Write down in your journal or Innovation Binder any thoughts or ideas you have about removing those obstacles so they no longer stunt your professional growth.

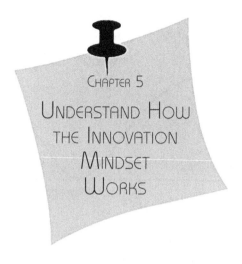

CHAPTER 5

UNDERSTAND HOW THE INNOVATION MINDSET WORKS

"There must be a beginning of any great matter, but the continuing unto the end until it be thoroughly finished yields the true glory."

~Sir Francis Drake

o become more innovative, it's important to understand what the innovation mindset looks like and how it works. I like to use Docherty's Innovation Mindset Model, developed by Mike Docherty, to illustrate this. Mr. Docherty wrote an article entitled, "Creating an Innovation Mindset," which brilliantly illustrates how the innovation mindset adoption curve works. He identifies five innovation mindset stages: dreaming, doubting, quitting or persevering, transforming, and championing.[6]

Docherty's Innovation Mindset Model

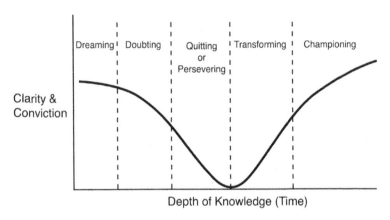

Image used with permission.

I've successfully applied these stages to my own experiences in becoming more innovative, and I want to show you how these five stages sometimes look and feel in action:

- **Dreaming** – This is where the process begins – with that great big idea that I know is the next best thing. I'm so excited about giving it a try, there's not much that could possibly stop me. Optimism abounds.

- **Doubting** – Inevitably, things don't go as planned, and I face the potential of a failed idea. It's not as easy as I thought it would be. At this stage, it's important for me to realize that failure is a natural and useful element of innovation. It forces me to learn from my failed effort and adapt the original idea or determine that it's time to try something else.

- **Quitting or Persevering** – This is the stage that truly separates innovators from dreamers. Am I willing to keep trying different strategies to make my idea happen if I believe deep in my gut that the idea still has potential? Or do I quit?

Sometimes quitting simply means the idea is not ready *yet*. Its time may come further down the road, or I may determine the idea wasn't as good as I originally thought it was. If I'm not making any progress and I feel like I'm beating my head against a wall, the best action may be to quit working on it *for a while* and give myself a chance to work on something different.

- **Transforming** – When I persevere through the implementation of my idea, I gain all of the benefits and rewards of the innovation experience. My confidence is then built upon depth of knowledge, experience, and the pride of having worked through the challenges that surfaced during the innovation process.

- **Championing** – When I repeatedly put this much effort into fighting through the challenges that lead to these transformational events, I always gain confidence! Typically, a healthy dose of recognition follows from my colleagues. But, as Mr. Docherty points out in his article, this also gives me the unique ability to champion continued innovation in myself as well as those around me. As I experience the implementation of my innovative ideas again and again, I gain a recognition and calmness about the trial and error process which is inherent in innovation. I also develop a clearer sense of when to pursue an idea further or when it's time to move on to another one.

Mr. Docherty's model helped me wrap my brain around the mental stages I would experience as I trained myself to become more innovative. Learning to persevere through failed efforts and self-doubt will help you build confidence in your ability to face fear head-on. These trials are all part and parcel of developing the innovation mindset. It's very easy to get discouraged or disheartened and to begin doubting your abilities. You may even be tempted to quit or abandon an idea if you don't understand what the process entails as you take an idea from concept to completion. But innovation sometimes requires years of practice, so you must get started!

> *"Take the first step in faith. You don't have to see the whole staircase, just take the first step."*
>
> ~ Dr. Martin Luther King Jr.

Some ideas we come up with will be better and more achievable than others. Sometimes great ideas start off sounding a little strange. We have to learn to suspend judgment until we have given those ideas time to mature and have had enough time to fully evaluate them. Over time, we may realize the idea we thought was so amazing in the "dreaming" stage isn't so amazing once we've put more thought into it. That's part of the innovation process.

Sometimes you have to develop a real depth of knowledge on a topic or idea before you discover the concept that later becomes the innovative idea. Only then can you implement that idea with confidence. Innovative thinking takes time -- time for ideas to percolate, time for experimenting with them to see what will work and what won't, and time for them to become fully brewed and ready to serve.

One thing I've learned about becoming *The Innovative Admin* is you must be prepared for things not to work the way you originally intended. We'll talk more about overcoming fear, self-doubt, and perceptions of failure in Chapter 18. For now, consider this: Thomas Edison and countless other inventors and innovators failed NUMEROUS times before their big ideas became a reality. It was what they *learned* from those failed attempts that ultimately put them in the position to become recognized for the inventions and ideas that *did* work.

Just because your first attempt to make something work may not be a success, it doesn't mean it's not worth pursuing at all. It doesn't even mean it was a failure. What it probably means is you need to re-engineer the initial concept and continue making some adjustments. What you learn throughout that process will be just as important on your road to becoming more innovative as any of the other things you will learn from this book.

PLAN OF ACTION:

☐ Think about an innovative idea you've had and implemented. How did the innovation mindset adoption curve apply to the implementation of your idea?

☐ Think about an idea you've had that did not work the way you intended. How did you handle it? What did you learn from it? How did it impact future ideas you tried to implement?

☐ Note your answers to the above questions in your journal or Innovation Binder.

CHAPTER 6

TURN YOUR
THINKING
UPSIDE DOWN

"Every activity is a process and can be improved."

~ W. Edwards Deming

One of the common elements you'll find among innovative minds is their ability to think differently. They regularly challenge the status quo – consistently asking "What if...?" Innovative thinkers are constantly looking for new and better ways of doing things that need to be done. You can train yourself to think differently, too.

One way you can do this is by establishing the habit of looking at everything you do with an investigative eye. Learn to challenge assumptions and exercise your imagination more. Practice generating ideas without judging them; then go back and evaluate them later. Consider what has worked well. What has not worked well? Why? Ask yourself if there were other ways you could have done things. What has become habitual because that's just the way it has always been done? Ask a lot of questions so you understand how things came to be done the way they are today, why they are that way, and how it might be improved. Use the history and apply that knowledge to the solutions you research and try.

Another way you can train yourself to think differently is to think about how another admin from a different company might look at your challenge or problem. What might that person suggest? Look around you and observe how others are doing things. How are others in different industries doing it? How can you connect what you've read or seen to what you're doing? Make a point of looking for the potential in new ideas and approaches even if they are very different from what you might normally consider.

Be willing to turn your thinking upside down when unanticipated events in your life throw you a curve ball. Many times we have to react quickly in order to address the immediate needs of the situation. But after the initial shock wears off, allow some time for reflection and see where the process or response may be improved. Why did you choose to handle it the way you did this time? How can you handle it better or differently the next time?

> *"Chaos often breeds life, when order breeds habit."*
>
> ~ Henry Adams

Learn From Bad Experiences

Sometimes, from our worst experiences come some of our most innovative solutions. A few winters ago, I slipped on the fresh snow and broke my left wrist. As an admin, you can imagine the wrench that threw into my life. How was I going to work? How could I type with a cast on my arm? How was I going to get to the office when I couldn't drive? I was forced to analyze how I worked, where I worked, and how I got where I needed to be each day. The results were quite astounding.

With a little bit of online research, I was able to find an ergonomic keyboard that was completely split in half so I could type normally with my right hand while typing vertically with my left hand. Since my left hand was casted, it was impossible to put it in a comfortable position to type on a regular flat keyboard. With my new split keyboard, I could type quite efficiently – cast and all!

Another amazing thing happened while I was laid up. Instead of clocking fewer billable client hours due to my broken arm, my billable hours actually increased! I was shocked. Upon further analysis, though, I realized I was spending more time focused on working during the day instead of driving to meet with people or meeting colleagues for lunch. I began using technology much more wisely by facilitating virtual meetings instead of face-to-face meetings. I changed the way I worked because of this challenge in my life, and as a result, my broken arm made me more efficient and more profitable.

When my arm healed and the cast was removed, I continued with my new habits and started looking at other areas in my home and work life where I could reevaluate and make some positive shifts as well. I was very thankful for this eye-opening experience to get my attention, challenge my thinking, and change my work habits.

Implement Review Meetings

Whenever I coordinate large events, I make it a standard operating procedure to do a post event wrap-up meeting. This allows you to sit down with all of the participants and analyze everything about the event – what worked well, what didn't work well, what you would do differently next time. It's also a great time to review any survey feedback from your event attendees to see what improvements they may have suggested. It's very important that you remain open to new and varied ideas and that you truly listen to the feedback and input from others if you want to expand your own thinking. When you incorporate a procedure like this into your regular routine even for the smaller events, projects, or activities you are involved in, it can provide insights you may otherwise overlook. Those insights contain the information you need to know so you can improve something the next time you do it. This can also help you turn your own thinking around.

Plan Ahead

When you are planning something, get in the habit of thinking about more than just your initial plan or idea. For admins, one perfect example of this is when you are coordinating travel arrangements. I don't know if there is another task in our day-to-day lives where there are more opportunities for things to go off course than with travel planning. Think about Plans B, C, D, etc., from the very beginning so you are prepared in case Plan A doesn't work out. Are there other flights available if the current flight is delayed or cancelled? Does the airport have conference facilities available if your stranded traveler needs to conduct a meeting virtually by phone or webcam? While it's impossible to prepare for EVERY possible contingency that may come up, this will help you be better prepared for the ones that do. It gets you in the habit of thinking ahead, thinking creatively, and being ready just in case.

A Mind-Stretching Exercise

Let me share a mind-stretching exercise I learned from small business coaching expert, Fabienne Fredrickson. When you are faced with something you think you can't afford or a problem you don't know how to solve, create a list of 50 ways you could make it happen. Write down every opportunity that could bring in money or provide a potential solution to the problem. Don't stop until you're written down *at least* 50 things. By doing this, you'll clear your head and make room for the new ideas to enter. You'll find that often the most obvious ways to accomplish something are the first things that pop into your head. However, after you get past writing down the first 10 to 15 things you think of, that's when you really have to stretch your thinking. You may not be able to come up with all 50 in one sitting. You may have to keep revisiting it. Once you have the list created, identify the six to nine items that will bring in the most money (or have the biggest impact on your problem) in the shortest time with the least effort. Then you take action on those things.

My husband and I did this exercise for a trip we wanted to take. Our list comprised of all the potential ways we could think of to pay for the trip *before* we took it. It was tough, and it took us several days to create our list. But it made us both think about some potential options in new ways we hadn't considered before. After about item number 20, we were getting pretty creative. That's the point...to stretch your thinking and train yourself to think in new ways to accomplish the objective at hand. It also shifts your thinking from the negative (we can't afford this) to the positive (here are several ways we CAN afford this).

I believe this same exercise can be applied to any problem you are trying to solve. Give it a try and see how it stretches your thinking and causes new innovative ideas to surface for you, too!

PLAN OF ACTION:

☐ Identify some areas of your personal or work life that you could look at in a new way.

☐ Take a look at all of the regular, routine things you do out of habit and see if there are some areas where you can turn your thinking upside down. Identify better, more efficient ways of doing them.

☐ Is there something that frequently bugs you? What is it? What are you currently tolerating that you'd like to change? Begin brainstorming ways you could turn your thinking upside down and resolve these situations.

☐ If you currently work on project teams or coordinate events and meetings, implement post event wrap-up meetings to evaluate what worked well, what didn't work well, and what could be improved for next time.

☐ Identify something you want to accomplish or achieve. In your journal or Innovation Binder, make a list of 50 ways you can achieve it in the next day, week, month, or year (depending upon the appropriate timeframe for the item you select). Repeat this exercise regularly for each new challenge you face or problem you want to solve.

CHAPTER 7

COLLABORATE
TO INNOVATE

*"Many ideas grow better when transplanted into another mind
than in the one where they sprang up."*

~ Oliver Wendell Holmes

One of the other key discoveries to becoming more innovative is the power of collaboration. The more you share knowledge, information, and ideas with others, the better your own ideas will become. Innovation develops when we exchange ideas between and among a diverse set of minds. It's the old adage, "two heads are better than one."

This happens for me all of the time. I have a concept that I share with a friend or colleague. They ask questions, add their own insights or ideas, and the original idea almost always becomes better – or sometimes takes a completely different direction – because I was willing to share it and collaborate with someone else.

Innovative thinking is a collaborative way of thinking; it's not territorial. You can't be an information silo where all of the knowledge, ideas, and creative thinking are exclusive to you. It has to be shared. If you want to attract other innovative minds to you, you must cultivate an innovative environment around you and be fully willing to collaborate and share with them also. Your unique abilities and signature impact become more powerful as you collaborate and share ideas with others and others share ideas with you.

> *"The whole is greater than the sum of its parts."*
> ~ Aristotle

In his book, *Stoking Your Innovation Bonfire,* Braden Kelley says:

> While many people give Thomas Edison, Alexander Graham Bell, and the modern-day equivalent, Dean Kamen, credit for being lone inventors, the fact is that the lone inventor myth is just that – a myth. All these gentlemen had labs full of people who shared their passion for creative pursuits.[7]

Who's in your innovation lab? Who *should* be in your lab?

I've worked in a lot of office environments where the atmosphere among the administrative staff wasn't always one of collaboration. Some people want to keep everything to themselves and not share it with anyone else. It's difficult to be the lone innovator in these situations. Sometimes you have to take the lead and demonstrate the behaviors and attitudes you want others to demonstrate. You have to stop worrying about what others are doing and work on yourself, sharing and collaborating when and where you can. Keep reinforcing the effectiveness of building a collaborative environment each time a collaborative effort is successful.

If you find you aren't making any headway and it's holding you back professionally, sometimes it becomes necessary to find a new or alternate environment that better supports your journey to becoming more innovative.

Even if your environment is not ideal at the moment, you can still develop a strong professional network that supports you outside of the immediate circle of admins you may work with daily. We'll talk more about this in Chapter 13 when we discuss developing your personal advisory board. For now, start thinking about who you want in your innovation lab with you. This will be one of the keys to your transformation into *The Innovative Admin*.

Also remember this: When you're working in collaborative environments, it's not always all about you. At times, it will be necessary and appropriate for you to give credit where credit is due. So be sure to recognize and acknowledge those who help you improve a concept through the collaborative process. This is a key component of building trust amongst your peers and fellow innovative collaborators. When you give them the recognition they rightly deserve, they will become some of your biggest fans and supporters.

I will also share this bit of advice in case you find yourself in a toxic environment and worry about someone else stealing your ideas and taking the credit. Be selective about whom you share your most innovative thoughts with. If you know someone has a habit of sabotaging others' plans or taking credit for ideas that aren't theirs, you may not want to include them in your innovation lab. This doesn't mean you don't share anything with them or bounce ideas off of them occasionally, but do so with caution.

What's important to remember is there are plenty of people out there who CAN and DO maintain confidences, will brainstorm with you, and will support you in your innovative pursuits. Find them. Share with them. Collaborate with them. And watch how the power of collaboration makes you not only a more innovative person, but builds alliances and relationships that are critical to your future and your success.

PLAN OF ACTION:

☐ Identify a list of positive, innovative people you would like to include in your new personal innovation lab. Write these down in your journal or Innovation Binder.

☐ What types of information, ideas, and resources do you currently share with others? How do you share them?

☐ What types of information, ideas, and resources could you share more frequently? The more you give, the more you receive.

CHAPTER 8

KNOW YOURSELF INSIDE OUT

"Know thyself."

~ Plato

The last foundational piece I'll talk about is the importance of knowing yourself inside out. This will serve you well in every aspect of your life, but it's also a very important component of becoming *The Innovative Admin*.

I've studied personality type, birth order, strengths, passions, and a variety of related concepts for much of my career. I treated this interest as more of a hobby at first. What I later learned was this is actually one of my strengths – specifically the individualization strength.[8] That's not surprising to me now that I understand what strengths are and how they develop in individuals. But professionally, this interest armed me with one of the most valuable databases of knowledge of all time: I know myself.

The more you know yourself, the more you know where you excel and where you have gaps or blind spots, what your strengths and weaknesses are, and how you normally behave in ideal settings versus what happens to you when stress is applied. The list goes on. This is vital information to have because it helps you navigate the waters of life with much clearer direction. The better you know yourself, the more precise you can be when asking for the help and resources you need to support what you're trying to accomplish. This is powerful data!

Can you articulate in clear terms:

- How you gather data or information?

- How you make decisions?

- How you communicate?

- What energizes you?

- What is your leadership style?

- What are your strengths?

- What are your passions?

- What is your personal mission?

- What are your personal and professional goals?

If you *can't* articulate your answers in clear terms, that may be a sign that you do not know yourself as well as you could. You must understand these parts of your personality well in order to effectively seek the counsel, collaboration, and insights of others who DO have those abilities to help you strengthen, expand, and stretch your own thinking.

In his book, *Magnificent Mind At Any Age*, Dr. Daniel Amen says:

> Passionate living is the soul of success and the hallmark of a magnificent mind. Without passion, little of consequence happens. Passion sparks the chemical factories deep in the brain, lighting the emotional fires

that turn us on.... Passion gives meaning and purpose to our lives. A magnificent mind requires directed passion, whether in raising healthy children, making a marriage amazing, thriving in your profession, or excelling at a hobby.[9]

When you ignite these circuits in your brain, they act as key drivers in your ultimate success. Consider the time and effort you put into getting to know yourself well a worthwhile investment.

There are several types of personality and related assessments I recommend to help get you started. Some are facilitated assessments and may have a fee associated with them. Others are available online or through the purchase of a book:

- StrengthsFinder 2.0 Assessment

- StandOut Assessment

- Myers-Briggs Type Indicator (MBTI)

- DiSC Assessment

- The Predictive Indicator (PI)

- Thomas-Kilmann Conflict Mode Instrument (TKI)

- 360° Reach Personal Branding Assessment

- {F} Score Brand Personality Test

- Innovator Mindset (IM) Assessment

- The Passion Test

See the Appendix for a list of recommended reading and resources related to these assessments.

After you've completed some of these assessments, be sure to keep a copy readily available in your Innovation Binder for reference and frequent review. You may also want to include copies in your professional portfolio for use at annual review time or for job hunting purposes. These assessment results will give you productive insights into what makes you the person you are today, letting you capitalize on your strengths and discover other areas where you could use additional support on your journey to becoming *The Innovative Admin*.

PLAN OF ACTION:

☐ Create a list of your own personal gifts, talents, abilities, skills, passions, and personality traits in your journal or Innovation Binder. Review any personality or skills assessments you've completed to jog your memory.

☐ Identify which personality or strengths assessment tools might help you better articulate what makes you uniquely you.

☐ Take a personality or strengths assessment and review your results.

    O Did the assessment accurately reflect or describe who you are?

    O What did you learn from taking the assessment?

    O Place your assessment results in your Innovation Binder.

Part 3: The Structural Components of Becoming *The Innovative Admin*

We've laid the foundation for becoming *The Innovative Admin*. Now it's time to look at the structural components that will help you build on this foundation. In the upcoming chapters, we're going to look at nine specific things you can do right now to begin making the transition from where you currently are to becoming *The Innovative Admin*:

- Start Journaling
- Create Space for Innovation
- Find a Hobby
- Develop Your Business Acumen
- Develop a Personal Advisory Board
- Tackle Technology
- Commit to Lifelong Learning
- Exercise Initiative
- Seek Challenges That Stretch You

"One's ability to generate innovative ideas is not merely a function of the mind, but also a function of behaviors. If we can change our behaviors, we improve our creative impact."

~ Clayton Christensen

CHAPTER 9

START
JOURNALING

"We cannot teach people anything; we can only help them discover it within themselves."

~ Galileo Galilei

D o you remember when your English teacher made you keep a journal? Many times, it was to encourage the art of writing, to help us learn how to express our thoughts, and to facilitate learning. A journal can help you do the same thing for yourself as an adult and in the professional world.

Journaling can be used as an important learning tool. When you capture on paper your ideas, thoughts, experiences, feelings, hopes, fears, and even opinions, you have the ability to review those reflections and potentially work through them, expand on them, and learn from them. Innovation requires time to allow thoughts to solidify and the best ideas to brew. Sometimes you have an idea but you don't have a clue what it means or what to do with it. Over time, as you continue to reflect on (or research) that idea more, it may evolve and turn into something even better – an innovative idea that you can implement. But unless you capture that initial idea somewhere – like a journal – it's likely to escape and disappear permanently.

There are many ways you can journal. There is no right or wrong way. Some people prefer paper, some prefer electronic methods; I actually recommend a system that integrates both paper and electronic so you can capture things quickly whether you're online or offline. The important element here is that you have a designated place where you regularly capture your thoughts and ideas so you can find them again later.

To get started, purchase a bright, cheerful looking journal or start your own Innovation Binder. You want your journal or Innovation Binder to make you feel good when you look at it and pull it out for use. Think of it as a personal treasure trove. I also recommend you have two journals – a larger one for regular journaling and a smaller one for carrying in your purse, bag, or briefcase to capture ideas when you're "on the go." If you use a paper planner, you may already use it as a tool to capture your ideas and lists of things you want to research later. If so, that's great. Just make sure you have them captured on stand-alone sheets that don't get removed when you move on to the next month. The idea is to have these pages always be accessible.

Next, setup an online folder or install a program such as Evernote or OneNote on your computer. These are great tools for capturing ideas as you find them online. Over time, you may also want to create subfolders with various categories to keep your ideas more organized.

Another option for journaling is audio journaling. With the assistance of a voice recorder (which you probably already have on your mobile phone, tablet or laptop devices), you can capture audio and save it to a file for future reference. If you want to take it a step further, you can purchase a tool such as the Livescribe™ smartpen.

With devices like this, you can capture not only audio but the notes you take with the pen can be converted to digital files also. Technology is truly amazing!

Although you certainly can use your electronic devices to capture ideas, there is something about physically writing and the journaling process that you will miss out on if you *only* use electronic tools to capture your thoughts. Many times you need space to doodle and draw to maximize your creative moments. Other times you need the speed and efficiency of an electronic tool. That is why I strongly recommend a combination of journaling methods to maximize your time and energy.

Once your paper and electronic journals are established, it's time to populate them. When you get an idea that you want to pursue further, capture it. When you see a product or website or have an idea that you want to research more, save it to your folder. If you find a resource you want to come back to later, write it down. This serves you in two ways: It eliminates the mental trauma of hoping you remember it later, and it also frees up valuable brain space for additional ideas to enter.

Writing down ideas and interesting tidbits becomes a great tool to help get the creative juices flowing and innovative solutions brewing. You may not use your journal every day, but you'll always know you have it right where you need it when a great idea hits you.

I use my journal to help me start thinking more innovatively on days I'm not feeling so inspired. I have some "starters" I use to get my mind recalibrated. They are:

- *Today, I am thankful for....* Write down at least five things.

- *What CAN I do today?* Write down the five things you CAN do to positively impact your life, your surroundings, your job, your family, your coworkers, etc. Then do them! This will help you focus on the positives in your life versus the negatives.

- ***Today, I accomplished....*** These also become super helpful when it's time to prepare for your annual performance review.

- ***Significant events in my life today (or this week) that impacted my actions and/or thoughts....***

- ***What I learned today....*** If you haven't learned at least one new thing today, then you need to pick up a book or get online and learn something new before you go to bed tonight.

- ***What single daily action(s) did I take today to move me toward my goals?***

I also use my journal as a place to write down my annual goals and the plan of action related to each goal so I can track my progress on a regular basis. My journal is my one-stop-shop for "all things admin."

Over time, your journal will become a place to unload your thoughts and inspire new ones. It will become a valuable tool packed full of tidbits and resources you can refer back to when you need them. It gives you a place to keep track of things and not only review where you've been, but map out where you want to go next.

> *"Ideas are fleeting; they must be captured. I find that some of the biggest payoffs from thinking occur when I record my thoughts."*
>
> ~ Mark Sanborn

PLAN OF ACTION:

☐ Purchase a bright, cheerful journal and a smaller journal or notepad for when you're "on the go" and/or create your own Innovation Binder. (Remember to download the complimentary cover, spine, and plans of action provided for you at www. TheInnovativeAdmin.com.)

☐ Setup an online folder or install an applicable software program where you can capture ideas when you are on your computer or electronic devices throughout the day.

☐ Create your first journal entry using the "starters" listed in this chapter.

☐ Commit to carrying the smaller journal with you all of the time.

☐ Commit to writing in your regular journal at least once a week – daily is encouraged.

CHAPTER 10

CREATE
SPACE FOR
INNOVATION

"Never mistake activity for achievement."

~ John Wooden

I f you want to become more innovative, you have to create the space and time for it. Innovation requires time for thinking and time for implementing. Our minds and bodies weren't designed to be in a constant state of tension and adrenalin rushes. It's not sustainable. You have to create a physical and mental environment where innovative thoughts can develop and you can experiment with implementing them by building innovation recharge time into your weekly schedule. Even if it's only five minutes a day to get started, *schedule it*! Then honor your commitment to this time to refresh your mental capacity each day.

Some days recharging may mean just sitting still and watching the birds outside your window or enjoying the flowers at the park. It could be as simple as reading the paper over lunch or after dinner. Other days, it may mean pulling out your journal and re-searching one of those ideas on the Internet. Stop by the public library or your local bookstore and find a book on the topic. You don't have to finish your research all in one visit, but get started. You can collect a lot of great ideas and information each day even if you only research, read, or listen to something for five to ten minutes. The more you do this, the more innovative your thoughts and ideas will become, because you're ADDING to the mental database on a regular basis instead of just pulling from it to accomplish the routine things you do each day.

I know you're busy. We all are. But you must make time for the things that are truly important to you.

Slow Down and Create a Change of Pace

Have you ever found yourself so caught up in the day-to-day tasks, "to do" lists, and activities that you feel like you're being driven by them instead of feeling in control of your surroundings? It happens to all of us. When it does, sometimes we have to manually press the reset button to get our focus back.

As I mentioned earlier, a few winters ago, I fell on a snow-covered parking lot and the "reset" button was pushed for me. I broke my left wrist, and I was thrust into the perfect environment for innovation – sitting still. I was very frustrated after my initial fall and diagnosis. Then, after a few days of sitting still, letting my head declutter, and allowing my life to slow down, I started to find myself thinking with a renewed focus. I began modifying the ways I completed tasks (because I was physically unable to do them the way I had before). In some cases, these new ways were actually better – they improved my life. I started asking people to come meet me for meetings instead of me driving to meet them. I was using my time more effectively and actually clocked more billable hours with a broken wrist than I had been billing prior to my fall.

Why hadn't I thought of these things before?

Why couldn't I see there was a better way to do this earlier?

Why did those things come to me when I could hardly type, I couldn't drive, and I was significantly limited in my activities for several weeks?

Here's why: For the first time in many months, I slowed down enough to allow myself to examine how I was working, where I was spending my time, and how I was accomplishing common everyday tasks. I had been forced to think and act differently.

Now, I don't recommend personal injury to get the process started, but there are numerous other ways you can manually press the reset button in your life and create an environment for innovation *without* injuring yourself. Let me share a few strategies you can implement to create space for innovative ideas to develop in your busy life.

Schedule Some Time Away From the Office

When was the last time you took some time off? When was the last time you took some time off without being connected to work or your work email? When was the last time you took a day or even a half-day off for professional development or personal enrichment? Sometimes you have to get out of your regular routine to recharge your body, mind, and spirit. When I take a vacation, it typically takes me two or three days to wind down before I am able to fully enjoy the time away. After I unwind and my head clears, I am able to absorb new information and start generating some new and exciting ideas. But this doesn't happen when I'm speeding along at 100 miles per hour on a regular basis.

One of the things I've also started doing is scheduling half day or full day excursions with a friend after I finish a big project or reach a milestone. This gives me something to look forward to and ensures that I slow down every so often to create the mental space for more innovative thinking. It's okay to be a little selfish here and take care of yourself first. It's the only way to ensure you stay charged and energized so you can continue to adequately care for those you support.

Create a Change of Space

When was the last time you rearranged your office? This might be tough if you work in cubeville, but look around and see what you *can* change up. You need to create a physical environment around you that supports innovation. Your environment sets the mood and tone for you.

If you want to be inspired, create an inspirational space around you. Frame some inspirational quotes and keep them visible. Maybe it's as simple as moving some plants or adding some greenery to your environment. What about rearranging the layout of the workspace around you? Remove the clutter from your desk and refresh your environment with some fresh flowers. Catch up on your filing. Add a desk lamp. I give you permission to go office supply shopping and buy yourself something new and fun! In fact, if you don't already have a white board, flip charts, or colored sticky notes easily accessible to do immediate brain dumps on paper when great ideas strike, those tools should be at the top of your shopping list. You can always add these to your journal or Innovation Binder later, but sometimes you need a larger space to visually organize the data in order for creative ideas to flow. Whatever you do, find a way to change your space to create a new environment that inspires a more innovative atmosphere for you.

Stop Multitasking, Start Concentrating

I hear a lot of admins tout their multitasking abilities. I used to be one of them. I will admit that multitasking has its place in some circumstances such as answering phones, rising to meet guests who have just walked into the office, and looking up a phone number for transferring a call – all at the same time. But if you are multitasking all of the time, I guarantee you're crowding out space for innovative ideas and thoughts to enter into your everyday environment. If there's too much happening all at once that requires your full attention, there's no room left for the good ideas to filter in. There's even less time to implement them. You're the one who suffers in the end because you're tired, burnt out, and left with little capacity for refueling.

> *"Multitasking arises out of distraction itself."*
>
> ~ Marilyn vos Savant

Start looking for ways to focus your attention on one thing at a time – even if it's only in 10-minute bursts. Become a master at overcoming interruptions. Team up with your coworkers. Create visuals that indicate you're in an interruption-free zone at various times throughout the day. Encourage "power project" hours for all staff during the day to help everyone become more focused, efficient, and productive.

When you stop multitasking, you can develop another important skill for all admins – active listening. Becoming a better, more focused listener will help you better address people's needs and make sure you get it handled right the first time.

Stop Watching (as much) Television

How many hours of television do you watch in a week? Or even in a day? What are you watching? If the average person watched just 10 minutes less each day over the course of a month, he or she would gain five hours of precious time for other activities such as reading, journaling, and just allowing your brain to rest and relax a bit. What most people find when they do this is they actually watch a lot less because they break the habit entirely. I'm not saying all television is bad. Watching a movie with your friends or family members can be relaxing and enjoyable, too. But, if you're looking for ways to create more innovation time in your day, this is a quick and easy way to grab a few minutes each week that may be slipping past you without you even realizing it.

Let Go of the Old

It has been my personal experience that in order to create space for something new in my life, I have to be willing to let go of something old that is no longer serving me as productively as it should be. This requires careful examination and thoughtfulness as I evaluate what I may need to change or let go. It may mean letting go of a regular networking activity or a professional affiliation. It may mean changing how I spend my time. It may mean examining my current habits and thought patterns. Once I've created the space for new things to enter, they always do. And they are almost always better in some way. The renewed energy, enthusiasm, and deeper insights that I gain are well worth it, too! But you must be willing to let go of the old if you want to create space for the new to enter.

PLAN OF ACTION:

☐ When would be the best time each day for you to schedule 5, 10 or 15 minutes of innovation time?

   ○ Schedule it now!

   ○ Honor your commitment.

   ○ Use the ideas in the upcoming chapters to determine what you should do each day during this time.

☐ Pull out your journal or Innovation Binder and start jotting down ideas on how you can create the space for innovation:

    ○ Professional development day or half day

    ○ Personal day or half day off

    ○ Vacation

    ○ Change your office space and environment

        ❐ Add or move plants or flowers

        ❐ Move furniture

        ❐ Organize your workspace

        ❐ Catch up on filing

        ❐ Add a desk lamp

        ❐ Add a new office supply item

        ❐ Other ideas: _____

    ○ Change your schedule

☐ Where could you cut down on some television time to create more innovation and personal recharging time in your day?

☐ Examine your habits, how you spend your time, activities you participate in, affiliations you have, etc. Are these things serving you as productively as they used to...or as they should? Identify areas where it may make sense to let go of the old to create space for something new in your life.

"Play is the highest form of research."

~ Albert Einstein

D o you have any hobbies or personal interests? When was the last time you spent any time enjoying or doing anything with it? If you don't have any hobbies, it might be time to find something you enjoy doing outside of work. Here's why: Learning something new typically requires you stretch yourself in a variety of ways – mentally, physically, emotionally. Hobbies are brain-builders. They are pleasurable. They jump-start chemical changes in the brain that trigger the imagination and help us solve problems.[10] Your favorite hobby affects the way your brainwaves function, so not only will your mind work more efficiently while you're enjoying the activity, but your brainwaves will *continue* to behave that way even after you put the project down.

Hobbies help your mind and body to relax. They add some variety to your life and enhance your wellbeing. The change of pace and activity helps you start thinking differently. Learning to think differently is required if you want to become an innovator.

Hobbies give you a chance to try out new things that you may not normally get to do in the course of your regular work. They give you a logical channel to pursue your passions and interests. Since you're the one choosing the hobby, it's usually an activity that provides enjoyment and an outlet for relaxation. With hobbies, you can learn new skills, explore different activities, find hidden talents, build confidence in yourself, meet new people, spend time alone or spend time with others – the opportunities are limitless.

Because hobbies are typically in an area where you have significant interests and talents, they help you develop the capacity for reaching beyond what you see on the surface and digging in to gain deeper insight. This capacity serves you well as you strive to become a more innovative thinker and problem solver in the workplace.

What have you always wanted to learn how to do? Have you always wanted to learn how to ride a motorcycle? Have you dreamed about becoming a ballroom dancer? What's stopping you? There's plenty of research to support the theory that a **new** hobby increases brain activity even more than an old one.[11] Learning new information and facing challenges push the mind into overdrive, and the stimulation pays dividends.

Don't use money as an excuse not to give your favorite hobby a try. Depending upon what it is, you'll likely find a lot of free resources online or at your local library. There are often a lot of low cost options available through local networking groups or continuing education programs at your local community college as well.

Many hobbies lend themselves to expanding your personal network at the same time. There are few hobbies that don't have an online forum or local networking group that meets to facilitate additional sharing and learning. There are book clubs for readers, quilting guilds for quilters, airplane clubs for pilots, stargazing groups for astronomers, checkers clubs for checkers players, scrapbooking events for scrap bookers, stamping parties for card makers...the list goes on. Remember: You must collaborate to innovate.

One of my personal hobbies is sewing. I love to create things with fabric. With each new home we've lived in over the years, one of my first projects after we move in has been designing and creating curtains for each room. I typically find curtain patterns I like and then modify them to accommodate my specific design preferences. I sketch the designs on paper and color them so I can visualize the final product. Then I begin calculating the amount of fabric and related materials I will need to complete the project. Sometimes they turn out perfectly. Other times, I'm forced to adapt and improvise throughout the project. My motto for craft and sewing projects is this: Each mistake or miscalculation is simply an opportunity to think of something even more creative to fix it or modify it. Sewing provides me a lot of enjoyment and diversion from my normal routine. But it's amazing how many times I've used the skills and abilities I've developed in becoming a seamstress in my administrative career. It has not only helped me with my project planning skills and taught me how to be more creative; it's given me the skills I have needed to create centerpieces, stage backdrops, and other event décor. You never know where you'll be able to transfer skills you gain from pursuing a personal interest into your career.

So what are some of the hobbies you once had that you've let slip by the wayside? Is it time to resurrect one or two of them? Is it time to find a brand new hobby – maybe something you've wanted to do for a while but didn't think you had time to pursue? I challenge you to pick one and schedule time for it within the next seven days. Even if it's only for 15 to 30 minutes, get started. I think you'll find it not only gives you something fun to look forward to, but it will give your brain something new to play with, too.

PLAN OF ACTION:

☐ List in your journal or Innovation Binder:

- What hobbies have you had in the past?

- Which of those hobbies would you like to start pursuing again?

- What new hobbies might you like to pursue?

☐ Schedule 15 to 30 minutes to spend on a hobby within the next seven days.

CHAPTER 12

DEVELOP YOUR BUSINESS ACUMEN

"It is no good trying to shine if you don't take time to fill your lamp."

~ Robert Frost

f I could help all admins develop one thing more fully, it would be stronger business acumen.

What is business acumen?

Business acumen is the understanding of how a business runs, what it takes for a business to make money, and the quickness and accuracy in understanding and dealing with a business situation in a manner that is likely to lead to a good outcome. Sometimes you'll hear this described as "business savvy" or "business sense."

The term "business acumen" can be broken down literally as a composite of its two component words: *Business literacy* is defined in the Society for Human Resource Management's Business Literacy

Glossary as "the knowledge and understanding of the financial, accounting, marketing and operational functions of an organization." The Oxford English Dictionary defines *acumen* as "the ability to make good judgments and quick decisions."[12] Business acumen is what you know about business and how you act upon – or implement – what you know.

Why is this important?

When you continually cultivate your knowledge and understanding of how businesses and organizations run at every level, you improve your ability to make good judgments and quick decisions each day. These abilities also help you think more innovatively about the challenges you may encounter and help you find the innovative solutions for solving them. Every action you take and each decision you make impacts another area in some way. You must understand how. If you don't understand, you must ask questions and do additional research so you can understand.

We are the eyes and ears of our executives and the teams we support. We are there to assist with connecting the dots between departments and team members to keep the communication and information flowing and the projects moving forward. If we don't understand the core business applications of sales and marketing principles, accounting practices, and operational functions within our respective companies, then we aren't as equipped as we need to be. When we overhear information being shared around us, we need to know how it potentially fits into other parts of the projects we are involved with or the initiatives our companies are pursuing so we can communicate potential concerns or assist with the flow of information appropriately. Even if you don't like numbers, you need to understand how to read financial documents. Even if the thought of selling something terrifies you, you must understand how the marketing and sales cycle works and how it impacts every other area within your company. Even if you think you already have a pretty good sense of how things run, there's always room to learn more – a lot more! When you understand how all of the pieces fit together, you understand how your company makes money, how it stays in business, and how you contribute to its success.

How do you strengthen your business acumen?

I had a client ask me one time, "How do you know *everything*? You're like super woman or something." I told her I make it my duty to know as much as I humanly can. It's the only way to stay relevant in my profession and provide significant value to those I support. But that got me thinking. How *do* I know what I know? What are the specific things I do to make sure I'm staying ahead of the curve? I will share several of the things I have done to develop my business acumen throughout this book. For this chapter, though, I want to focus on the PRIMARY thing you can start doing **immediately** that will make a HUGE impact in your business education and exposing yourself to innovative concepts:

Read. READ. READ!

Online, offline, and everywhere in between! Read books. Read newspapers. Read magazines. Read junk mail. Read blogs. Read news stories via smartphone apps. Download free reports off of websites. Scan the content on social media sites such as Twitter, LinkedIn, and Facebook. **Read and learn!**

Who has time for all of that reading, you ask? YOU DO when you MAKE THE TIME to do it. There is no substitute; you MUST read.

I'm not suggesting you read everything you touch cover to cover. I also understand that this is easier for some personality types to become comfortable with than others. But the more you read, the better you will get at reading more often.

When I'm reading, I'm scanning for content that will help me better understand today's business environment, give me a deeper understanding of industries I support or have supported in the past, and educate me on new technologies and emerging marketing practices on the web. I scan the random magazines and junk mail that comes across my desk just to see what's in them. I find marketing ideas for clients and professional organizations I belong to. I learn about best practices for HR. I discover innovative ways to incorporate social media into marketing campaigns. I find new ideas on how to use social media for building corporate brands and promoting products and services online. I uncover new resources for event planning and meeting coordination. I learn how to use software programs more efficiently. The list is endless.

I want to share some excerpts from Dan Kennedy's book, *No B.S. Time Management for Entrepreneurs*:

You MUST read a lot to succeed. Here are the reasons:

(1) Varied, diverse input, ideas, viewpoints, life stories, examples, all the essential raw material poured into your subconscious mind, for it to sift, sort, try matching up with other puzzle pieces it already has, so it can occasionally yell "Eureka!" and hand you something profitable – without daily flow of new stuff, it just sleeps....

(2) Without exposure to others' thinking, your own range of thought shrinks. Soon you are a mental midget. Your range of thought narrows, like your range of motion shrinks if you don't move and stretch.

(3) You can't stay current. I read a monstrous amount and I still can't stay current. If you're not reading a book or two, a dozen magazines, a few newspapers, and a few newsletters every week, you must be way, way, way behind. Pretty soon, your conversation reveals you a dinosaur.

(4) If you have kids, you want to set a decent example for them.[13]

These principles apply for any person who wants to be successful in any area of life. Dan Kennedy also has a list of questions you can use to quiz yourself at the end of each week to help direct your focus for the week ahead.[14] I've adapted his list a bit so it's more directly applicable to administrative professionals:

What do you know this week that you didn't know last week about...

- Your company?

- Your industry as a whole?

- Your company's competitors?

- Your company's customers or clients as a group?

- Your company's top 10, 20, or 30 customers or clients? (If you don't know who these are, then find out. You should know this!)

- One of your company's clients or customers, individually?

- One of the top leaders in your field or profession?

- Societal, cultural, or economic trends that may affect your company's business?

- A "success" topic – personal finance, self-motivation, time management, project management, staying organized?

- A "marketing" topic – direct-response advertising, social media marketing, copywriting that sells, direct mail, the Internet?

- A person, event, or topic in the current news of great interest or importance to your company's clientele?

- A "method" – a means, process, technique of doing something useful to you, whether learning how to do a component of your job more efficiently or using a piece of software more effectively?

Kennedy says if you actually discipline yourself to get one answer to each question worth putting down in writing just once a week, after a year, you'll be **624** big steps ahead of your peers and competitors. That is an AMAZING statistic! And it will help you STAND OUT as an administrative professional in ways you never imagined.

Sometimes it is necessary to spur your own innovative processes with external stimuli. Here's a list of ideas to help get you thinking about what you can find to read starting today. This list is by no means exhaustive.

Book topics

- Business practices
- Marketing
- Leadership
- Entrepreneurism
- Negotiation
- Self-motivation
- Career development
- Human resources
- Economics

Newspapers

- Local newspapers
- Regional business journals
- National newspapers

Tip: Smartphone and tablet device apps are great for staying current with national newspapers and news organizations.

Magazines

- Event planning and trade show publications
- Industry related
- Profession related
- Business related
- Hobby related

Tip: Search online for free magazines you can access directly from the Internet.

Websites and Blogs

Search topics of interest to you. When you find good sites, bookmark the site or subscribe to their RSS feeds. RSS stands for really simple syndication. It simplifies how website and blog owners can automate sending their content updates to you and saves you the time of having to visit their sites daily looking for updates when you sign up for their RSS feeds.

A blog is simply an interactive website with regularly updated content that you can comment on and subscribe to by an RSS feed so you receive their updates via email or your RSS reader.

The alternative to subscribing to RSS feeds is to create a favorites list called "Reading Materials" in your web browser, save the site as a favorite in your web browser, and scan the bookmarked sites and their associated blogs regularly. Online news sources are useful, too.

Here are some websites to get you started.

- www.SmartBrief.com
- www.BusinessInsider.com

- www.Entrepreneur.com

- www.Mashable.com

- www.wsjonline.com

- www.Forbes.com

- www.AMAnet.org

- www.hubspot.com

- www.AliBrown.com

- www.ClientAttraction.com

- www.SocialMediaExaminer.com

- www.Adminology.org

- www.OfficeDynamics.com

- www.AllThingsAdmin.com

Many sites have daily or weekly email bulletins (e.g., enewsletters or ezines) they can send to you also if you sign up for them. Subscribe to electronic newsletters related to the industry in which you work, administrative resource websites, hobby related websites, or your specific areas of expertise. Most of these are free and provide great content and resources. I recommend creating a separate email address solely for developing your business acumen, which also keeps your work email less cluttered. If you don't have time to scan and read the websites or email bulletins on a daily basis, just do it once or twice a week. This might also be a great evening or weekend activity to substitute for a few minutes of television watching time each week.

Social Media Sites

If you're using social media sites like LinkedIn, Twitter, or Facebook, you can search for specific topics or industries.

- **LinkedIn** – Join some profession- or industry-specific groups. You'll be amazed at the information that is shared in these forums. You can also ask questions and search for resources.

- **Facebook** – Research your customers, clients, and competitors here. See what they're doing and share what you learn with your team.

- **Twitter** – This is one of the most under-utilized resources by admins. Search for your customers, clients, and competitors here also. Search for resources to make you more effective as an admin (e.g., career topics, time management, leadership, etc.).

Find key influencers on your social media sites to "connect" with, "follow," or "like" who post links to great information and resources. The biggest advantage to using social media is that you can do it in very little time at ANY time of the day. Almost every social media site is set up to work with mobile devices, so you can access it on the go! You can find a lot of free teleseminars (training by phone) and webinars (training by computer) using search functions on social media sites.

The thing about reading is this: The only one who can do it for you is YOU. And you have to make the time to do it. It can be squeezed into your day with amazing ease when you concentrate on making it a priority in your daily and weekly routine. Here are a few simple ways to fit it into your day:

- **Take a book or magazine with you to read over lunch.** If you don't normally take a lunch break, start now! Even if you only get 30 minutes, start with that. Feeding your body physically (with food) and mentally (by reading) will give you the physical nourishment and mental invigoration you need to get you through the rest of the day more successfully.

- **Listen, read, or watch while you exercise** (if safe to do so). Make a workout fly by while filling your mind with useful information. With books on audio CD, books on e-readers, and training via podcasts and MP3 downloads, this is one area in which I encourage multitasking. It's a great way to use one habit to motivate and facilitate the other, and it helps your exercise sessions go more quickly, too.

- **Keep CDs, books, or other publications with you at all times.** When you're waiting to pick up family members from their activities during the week, you can skim through industry magazines that you receive but rarely get time to review. Instead of listening to annoying radio commercials while you commute, fill your time with an audio training course. If you don't have time to read like you want to, always keep a book with you in case of downtime. Even reading just a page or two will benefit you.

With all of the media available, there's no excuse. You can benefit from them and stimulate your capacity for innovation at the same time. You may not be able to do each one of these every day, but you CAN do at least one each day. Be resourceful. Find the ways that work best for you. Then do them consistently!

I don't accomplish the same amount each day. Some weeks it's easier to do than others. But reading is a habit you CAN develop. Once you do, your business acumen will become stronger by the day and you will become increasingly more valuable to everyone you support – now and in the future!

PLAN OF ACTION:

☐ Identify which websites or blogs you find beneficial for your industry, profession, hobbies, and interests in your journal or Innovation Binder. Subscribe to a few RSS feeds so you can receive regular updates.

☐ Identify enewsletters or ezines related to your industry, profession, hobbies, and interests, and subscribe to them via their websites.

☐ Research social media sites for key influencers in your industry, profession, hobbies, and interests.

    O   Follow, like, or connect with them.

    O   Observe what they are sharing and posting.

    O   Consider joining social media networks you may not be using yet, such as Twitter, LinkedIn, or Facebook.

☐ How can you better utilize your lunch break?

☐ What could you listen to, read, or watch while you exercise?

☐ What could you safely listen to or read when you have downtime, like riding (not driving!) in the car, commuting to work on a train, etc.?

☐ Review the list of questions provided in this chapter to quiz yourself at the end of each week to see what you've learned about your company, profession, industry trends, etc. Record the answers in your journal or Innovation Binder.

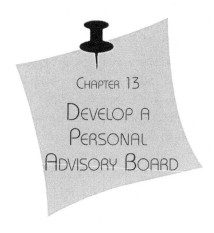

CHAPTER 13

DEVELOP A
PERSONAL
ADVISORY BOARD

"Surround yourself only with people who are going to lift you higher."

~ Oprah Winfrey

It's important to surround yourself with wise, innovative advisors if you want to become a more innovative person yourself. Do you have a personal advisory board to help you through making difficult decisions, evaluating new opportunities, or pursuing professional goals? If not, how do you develop one?

Your personal advisory board may include coworkers, colleagues from professional associations, friends, people you follow on the web, or even family members. Think about who inspires you to view things in different ways. Who challenges you to pursue new opportunities? Who do you admire and why? When you need solid advice, whom do you call? When you are looking for productive feedback, to whom do you turn? These are probably some people you should consider spending more time with either in person or virtually. Innovation is contagious.

What is a Personal Advisory Board?

A personal advisory board is a small group of objective people who know you well, who are interested in your personal and professional success, and who are able to help you think. They can help accelerate your success and take some of the fear and uncertainty out of the process. A good personal board will provide both support and wisdom for you as you pursue your personal and professional goals. If you want to become more innovative, make sure you include innovative people on your personal advisory board.

How Do I Select My Advisors?

Over the past several years, I have purposefully spent time developing a personal advisory board and identifying criteria for whom I should include. As my career has advanced, having a personal advisory board has become more and more critical to my personal and professional success. I'm very selective about whom I place on my personal board, though. Here are some of the criteria I consider:

- Who sharpens me?

- Who inspires me to achieve more?

- Who supports, encourages, and pushes me to keep climbing and reaching to achieve the goals I have set for myself?

- Who brings new perspectives and ideas into my life?

- Who stretches my thinking?

- Who is willing to offer truly constructive criticism when I need it?

- Who is willing to tell me directly that he or she thinks I have a bad idea or am headed in the wrong direction?

- Who brings a completely different background and set of experiences into my thoughts and awareness?

- Who knows and understands my strengths, weaknesses, and personality type?

- Are they emotionally tied to the outcome of my decisions? Or can they be objective?

- Are they positive and forward thinking?

These are the people that I want to surround me and support me no matter what comes my way. Jim Rohn, an American entrepreneur, author and motivational speaker said, "You are the average of the five people you spend the most time with." So you want to put careful thought into who those people are. Fabienne Fredrickson, a small business coaching expert, says your results in life are directly proportionate to the expectations of your peer group, so find a high level mentor if you want to play a higher level game. The bottom line is this – *with whom you spend time and surround yourself matters!*

I have both men and women on my personal advisory board. I have administrative professionals, business owners, financial and legal professionals, and executive/success coaches. Their educational backgrounds vary. Their experiences overlap in some areas and significantly vary in others. It's a fantastic mix of trusted advisors.

This criteria is also a component of how I evaluate which networking opportunities I participate in. If I am the average of the five people I spend the most time with, I'd better make sure they are five outstanding people. If I'm going to invest my valuable time to attend a networking function, it had better provide a significant return on my time investment. This gives you some concrete factors to evaluate so that you make good choices not only about whom you spend time with but *how* you spend your time with them. I like to refer to this as strategic networking.

Strategic networking is worth keeping in mind as you socialize at the office, too. Casual socializing is important for building rapport with your coworkers. This is an important part of what effective admins do. However, if you find casual socializing is eating into significant amounts of your day or draining your energy, it may be time to make some adjustments. Are you surrounding yourself with wise advisors in your casual office interactions? This gives you additional criteria by which you can evaluate even workplace socializing.

Meeting and Communicating with My Advisors

Most of my personal advisory board members do not know they hold that "unofficial" position. I do communicate with each of them regularly, though, by phone, email, social media, and getting together for coffee or lunch. I share what I'm doing and the goals I'm pursuing. I share my successes and my challenges. I bounce ideas off them. They help keep me accountable to my timelines. One of my board members is so in tune with who I am and what I'm trying to accomplish, she sends me ideas and supporting information to keep me inspired on an almost daily basis. I love that! Her random thoughts and tidbits of inspiration have been extremely valuable to me. In turn, this inspires me to be the type of person others would want to have around them and supporting them as well. It's contagious.

Giving Back to My Personal Advisory Board

As my personal advisory board members support, encourage, challenge, and inspire me, I realize this is not a one-way street. I am constantly thinking about ways I can add value to their personal and professional lives as well. I want to meet the same criteria as I have set for my own personal advisory board for my friends and colleagues. I also make sure I show my sincere appreciation for them. This can take the form of small gifts, or books, or even by treating them to coffee or lunch, and saying thank you verbally and in writing when appropriate.

There's an old adage, "There's wisdom in a multitude of counselors." Surround yourself with many wise advisors, and you'll reap the benefits of their wisdom and insights as you actively pursue your personal and professional goals. Your success as an innovator depends on it!

PLAN OF ACTION:

☐ Develop a list of names in your journal or Innovation Binder that you'd like to have on your personal advisory board.

☐ Make a list of ways you can more regularly interact with, spend time with, or learn from some of those people (e.g., schedule a lunch date, pursue a formal mentoring relationship, join a professional association, attend networking events, follow or connect with people on social media sites, attend training sessions they provide, read their blogs and books).

☐ Make a commitment to yourself to do at least ONE thing this week that causes you to interact in some way with one of your personal advisory board members. Repeat weekly.

CHAPTER 14

TACKLE
TECHNOLOGY

*"The world hates change, yet it is the only thing that has
brought progress."*

~ Charles Kettering

Where would we be without technology? When I was a child, I remember watching with awe as my mom typed on our family's manual typewriter. Her fingers flew over the keys so quickly and she'd swing the carriage return back line after line without missing a beat. Hard as I tried, I could never make it look so smooth and effortless – or error free. Then we got our first electric typewriter. What a treat! Not only did it return the carriage for me with the push of a button, it had the correction tape built into the ribbon. What a machine! And I could finally type with some speed and precision thanks to this technological dream.

Fast-forward to today and the electric typewriter is a relic. Technology has advanced at lightning speeds. Now we can not only carry our laptops, iPads, smartphones, MP3 players, and more with us wherever we go, we can even connect to the Internet from almost any location we are in! Working virtually has become much simpler and more mainstream using cloud computing and Internet-based collaboration platforms.

Technology is NEVER going to stop advancing, so if you think you know all you need to know to do your job, think again. Technology touches everything we do in some way, and that's not going to change. So don't let technology scare or intimidate you. MASTER IT. Conquer it. The funny thing about technology is the more you use it, the more user-friendly it becomes. In order to unleash your innovative ideas, you need to have an understanding of how technology may be incorporated into the implementation of them.

Just a few years ago, most of us could have never imagined the volume of products, services, games, entertainment, and countless other tools that could be delivered to our fingertips with the simple installation of an application (also called an "app") on a smartphone or tablet device. If you don't embrace technology and each advance it makes, you'll fall behind very quickly. And the only thing worse than not staying current is losing ground.

One of the best ways to embrace advances in technology is to get your hands on the new technology as soon as you can. That might mean going to the local office supply store to test out a display model or finding a friend or coworker who can give you a quick demonstration. I remember when one of my executives handed me his Blackberry and asked me to setup his email. I had never touched one before in my life. I went online to search for some user guides. I called a couple of people I knew who used them to ask a few questions. I started working with it a bit myself to see how it worked. A few hours later, I had successfully setup his three email accounts on his new Blackberry. I also made some notes and documented the procedure in case I ever had to do it again – which I did a few years later. This hands-on experience was the best teacher, though.

Another way to tackle technology is to be aware of which software packages you use and stay on top of updates and new versions that roll out. Pursue the training required to master it BEFORE you need it. A lot of software companies will offer a beta version of new software that you can demo or try for free even before the initial release to the public. While your corporate information technology (IT) department may frown upon doing that on your work computer, you can test them out on your home computer so you're already a proficient user when the upgrade finally rolls out at the office. Many of these same software companies even offer online training tutorials and resources free of charge to help get you started. (YouTube.com is packed full of free training and demonstrations if you search for them.) Most IT departments will look for internal staff to help beta test software for the company before it's rolled out company-wide. Talk with your IT staff and find out how you can be included in those opportunities. You know your coworkers are going to be asking you questions about the software when they start using it anyway, so get a head start and begin mastering it as soon as you possibly can.

Research what skills you need to learn to remain competitive and LEARN THEM. Electronic devices and communication are continually becoming technology and software based. As I write this book, social media use continues to be a growing trend. Admins need to learn how social media marketing works, how it can be used, which sites are best for personal and business use or both. Consider website development training – basic website development, basic HTML, and blogging. Almost every company is utilizing or shifting to web-based, collaborative platforms, and you need to understand how to use these technologies. Master the core Microsoft Office software programs, then get started learning the premium suite programs that accompany it. If some of these skills haven't shown up in your job description yet, it's just a matter of time before they do.

I'd also encourage you to talk to recruiters or human resources professionals and ask them what skills their clients are looking for. You need to regularly comb through the help wanted ads and job boards to see what skills are in demand for the types of positions you desire. Ask your executives what skills they'd like you to develop further as you continue to support them. Better yet, assemble your list and give them some ideas of what you'd like to pursue and why.

I regularly hear admins fret and worry about not being able to stay caught up with technology, but when I ask them when the last time they took a class or attended training was, many haven't pursued a single activity. Training is not your company's responsibility. It's yours! It's nice if you can gain corporate support to help finance your training needs, but even if your company can't, you must still pursue it on your own.

There are technology training options available to you at ALL price points. While some of the higher cost training programs may not be an option if you are the one financing them, there are still lots of economical and no cost training options around if you know where to look. If you utilize social media wisely, you can find a lot of training for free. Here are just a few resources to check out for the training you need:

- Local chapters of professional organizations (e.g., International Association of Administrative Professionals)

- Conferences and workshops

- Community college continuing education programs

- Online webinars and teleclasses

- Networking groups

- Chamber of Commerce

- Local business building organizations or small business incubators

- Local libraries

- Blogs and websites

- Social media sites (e.g., LinkedIn.com, Twitter.com, Facebook.com)

Start to watch the calendar of events section of any local newspaper or advertiser insert and you'll start seeing opportunities you never knew were out there – many for just the cost of dinner and your time!

Don't let technology be the big scary monster in the corner. Instead, make it your friend and embrace it wholeheartedly. I guarantee the more time you spend with it, the more fun and useful it will become to you in every area of your life.

PLAN OF ACTION:

☐ Identify where you may lack technological knowledge.

☐ Do some research on the best training options available to you for correcting that deficit.

☐ In your journal or Innovation Binder, map out a personal technology training timeline for the next 12 months that facilitates filling the knowledge gaps you have.

> *HINT: This is another great goal to work into your annual performance review at work. It may also help you gain your employer's financial support for taking additional courses.*

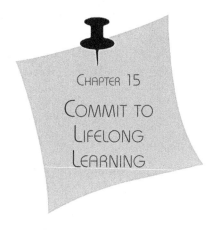

CHAPTER 15

COMMIT TO
LIFELONG
LEARNING

*"I don't divide the world into the weak and the strong, or the
successes and the failures... I divide the world into the learners
and the nonlearners."*

~ Benjamin Barber

Whether you're looking for a job, pursuing a promotion, or trying to change habits and thinking patterns as you become more innovative, becoming a lifelong learner will serve you well. Developing your business acumen requires constant learning. No matter how indispensable we think we've made ourselves in our executive support roles, THERE ARE NO GUARANTEES. Companies get bought. Companies get sold. Executives transfer. Departments get outsourced. Work cultures shift. Personal obligations and preferences change. It's not personal, it's business. But if "business" happens to you, are you prepared?

What are you doing *right now* to make sure you continue to remain competitive in the changing environments that surround you?

What are you doing to specifically develop your business acumen every day?

Do you know what additional skills you need to be developing if you plan to work in the administrative profession for another 5, 10, or 15 years?

> *"The day you stop learning is the day you start dying."*
>
> ~ Unknown

We talked about the status quo mindset in Chapter 4, and I shared some of the statements I commonly hear from those stuck in status quo mindsets. In this chapter, I want to take a closer look at some of these statements, and point out where this thinking falls short.

Statement: "I don't have to know that to do my job. We have a travel department that handles it for us."

Analysis: What if your travel department is eliminated? What if your next company doesn't have a vendor or internal department for you to rely on? You need to know how to do what your travel department does because one day you may *become* the travel department! What are you doing to learn these skills now?

Statement: "Nothing in that training applied to me, I don't have to do that on my job."

Analysis: Maybe you don't have to do it *yet*! But are you planning for your next career move? What if you need that information or skill set in the future? Is your mental database fully populated so you're ready to hit the ground running when you DO NEED that knowledge?

Statement: "I would never use that in my current position."

Analysis: Perhaps you do not get to do that kind of work because you don't have the skills to do it yet? Have you asked if you can add new responsibilities to your position? What if you change jobs and need to know it there?

Statement: "We can't use Facebook or Twitter at work. They have those sites blocked."

Analysis: In the early days, the Internet used to be blocked at work for most people, too. Remember those days? Social media accessibility at work will continue to evolve. Admins are being asked to help coordinate those efforts. Do you know the difference between each social networking site and how to use it to positively market your company?

Statement: "We hire an outside firm to do our website design work."

Analysis: How much money and time could you save your company on website updates if you could do the quick updates yourself instead of waiting for someone else to do it for you? As things become more web-based, basic HTML and website development skills will be necessary for employees at all levels.

Statement: "I'm planning to retire in just 'X' years, so I won't need that."

Analysis: What happens if you get laid off before your retirement date? Are your skills current and relevant enough to get you another job at the same pay rate until you can retire? When is the last time you took a training course to update your skills?

There are a lot of professionally limiting beliefs in those statements. The most common element present in each one of those statements is complacency. Complacency is a feeling of contentment or self-satisfaction, especially when coupled with an unawareness of danger or trouble. Complacency can be a career killer if you don't guard against it.

So how do you avoid complacency that comes with the status quo mindset?

Become a persistent learner in every area of your life.

Learn it BEFORE you need it. Pursue learning new things for fun! Don't wait to be asked to add a skillset to your résumé. Take a class online or through your local community college related to accounting, marketing, leadership, project management, improving your writing skills, or becoming a better negotiator. Beta test new software releases. Develop your website and HTML skills. These are all things that can only increase the opportunities available to you – both personally and professionally. At the same time, the more you develop your skills in these areas, the more confident you will become in trying new things and implementing these new ideas into your daily work and routine. This is where you'll begin to experience the power of innovation in your career.

> *"If you will spend an extra hour each day of study in your chosen field, you will be a national expert in that field in five years or less."*
>
> ~ Earl Nightingale

In one of my executive assistant roles, I had the opportunity to take a database course through a local training center. When I returned to the office, I looked for ways that I could use this new program so I wouldn't forget what I had learned. Our sales and marketing team coordinated annual incentive golf events for all of the top sales people in our company, so I volunteered to create an event database to track all of the details related to the event. It started out small, but it quickly became a big project as we kept adding to the database design and functionality each year. My database became an ongoing tool the event coordinators used to run that annual event. This opened the door for additional database projects and training opportunities.

Have you considered pursuing a college degree or professional certificate program? Sometimes you have to be willing to ASK for the training you need. One of my colleagues often says, "Do you wait for your boss to ask you if you want to take a vacation? No. So why do you expect them to ask you if you want to take some training classes?" Don't wait for your executive to ask you; be proactive, assemble your list of training needs, and present it to your executive for consideration. And don't forget to take advantage of any tuition reimbursement benefit programs that your company may also offer. (See the Appendix for additional details on how to build a business case for training requests.)

Options abound, but you have to embrace lifelong learning and seek them out! One of my favorite quotes comes from business strategist Sherese Duncan:

*"In order to think out of the box, realize there is **no** box."*

There is nothing stopping you from learning something new – except you! Get comfortable with being outside of your comfort zone. That's also where you will find additional insights and inspiration in your quest to become more innovative.

When you're happy in your current position or with your current company, it's hard to imagine being laid off or suddenly in a position where you need to look for a new job. But business happens, and innovative, proactive, success-minded administrative professionals are prepared. They have learned the skills they need and have proof of their abilities. You may be a few years from retirement with no plans to work anywhere else, but things can change in an instant. No matter what your career objectives are or how close to retirement you may be, you still need an updated résumé, a professional portfolio, a fully developed and functioning network, and a career plan of action. You also need all the advantages that becoming a lifelong learner provides.

To quote one innovative admin I know:

"Be savvy about what you want. Be honest.
If you hate being an admin — then get out of the profession.
If you love it and want to continue to grow — you
have to do the legwork.
The job market is too tight for sitting back and hoping
whatyou've done in the past will be enough. Get busy!"

~ Kemetia M K Foley

Real growth requires hard work and effort. If you're too comfortable, you're not growing. No matter what the economy does, there are always companies out there looking for competent, qualified administrative professionals. Make sure you are one of them.

PLAN OF ACTION:

In your journal or Innovation Binder, identify some areas where you'd like to learn something new, continue developing your skills, and stretch your comfort zone. Don't limit yourself only to skills you need at the office or for career development. Open your mind and yourself to new things outside of your job as well, and it will open doors for you in unexpected ways. Here are some ideas to get you brainstorming:

○ Archery

○ Ballroom Dancing

○ Blogging

○ Cartoon Drawing

○ Cooking Classes

○ Community / Charity Events

○ Event Planning

○ Foreign Language(s)

○ Gardening

○ Job Hunting

○ Leadership Development

○ Management

○ Multi-media PowerPoint Presentations

○ Music Appreciation

○ Outdoor Activities

○ Pilates

○ Professional Association Membership

○ Public Speaking

○ Scrapbooking

O   Social Media

O   Software Programs

O   Sports

O   Stamping

O   Travel Planning

O   Website Development

O   Woodworking

O   Others: _____

☐ Do some research to find out where you can learn more about the areas you have selected (e.g., online courses, community college classes, local retailers, books, blogs/websites, seminars, associations, people you know).

☐ Make a commitment to yourself to do at least ONE thing this week to further your knowledge in one of the areas you identified (e.g., read a book on the topic, subscribe to a free newsletter, sign up for a class). Then repeat this again next week and the next week...you get the idea.

☐ For added accountability, choose one area to include in your goals for the upcoming year when you have your annual performance review.

CHAPTER 16

EXERCISE
INITIATIVE

"Initiative is doing the right things without being told."
~ Elbert Hubbard

To become *The Innovative Admin*, you must be able to take action and get things done without waiting for someone else to tell you what to do, or when and how to do it. When you have ideas you want to implement, you need to know how to take the initiative to implement them. But like anything, if you aren't comfortable doing this or you work for someone who doesn't encourage you to take the initiative, it can be challenging.

What is initiative? Initiative is that introductory step or action you take when you implement an idea. It's personal action. Initiative starts with you and what you do to *responsibly* prepare for and act upon an opportunity or idea. It's you initiating things independently. You see what needs to be done and you do it.

If you are not used to regularly exercising initiative, you need to start small by gently asking your supervisor or making a recommendation at an appropriate time. As you gain confidence over time, you shift toward sharing what you intend to do and then reporting back after the idea is implemented. Eventually your awareness of your environment will tell you when you need to get approval first and when you can just simply take the initiative and implement.

In his book, *The 8th Habit*, Stephen Covey goes into a lot of detail on learning how to become more self-empowered to take more initiative. He outlines the seven levels of initiative or self-empowerment as follows:

Level 1)   Wait until told
Level 2)   Ask
Level 3)   Make a recommendation
Level 4)   "I intend to"
Level 5)   Do it and report immediately
Level 6)   Do it and report periodically
Level 7)   Do it

Mr. Covey also adds this, "The key question is always, What is the best thing I can do under these circumstances?"[15] It's up to you to make that evaluation and act accordingly.

Choosing which level of initiative to use requires understanding your circumstances and exercising good judgment. But as you begin to successfully exercise more initiative, and trust builds between you and those you support, you become more self-empowered and have the power to positively lead and influence others with your innovative ideas. When you ask for feedback along the way, you'll be able to gauge how you're doing as well.

Here is an example of exercising initiative in my own career that may be a great place for you to begin exercising initiative in your position. When I was working corporately, I never started a new administrative position that had a procedures manual already developed for the position. So I always made this my first priority after my training period was finished. The notes I took while I was being trained combined with all of the information and resources I had been given during my orientation were the starting point of this new "admin binder" or procedures manual for my position. I would continue to add to it as I came across other things that should be included over time. When I would share this binder with my executives, they were always amazed that I had taken the initiative to put this valuable tool together. This simple action led to other department heads sending their new admins to spend a few hours training with me during their first few days on the job. I communicated updates or changes in my procedures to these other admins as I updated my own binder.

In order to keep all of the administrative assistants in my division connected and communicating department specific policy and procedure updates, I initiated quarterly admin lunches. We had to get approval for the lunch meeting to be expensed, but it was an easy decision for the executives we were supporting because they could already see the value in what we were proposing. Not only did we all get out of the office once a quarter, we all stayed more involved with the interworking of our individual departments which, ultimately, helped the flow of work and communication between departments as well. Because I had taken the initiative to create my original admin binder and then chose to share it with others in my division, it facilitated my becoming recognized as an administrative leader within my company.

Initiative is a required component of innovation. Innovation doesn't occur without implementation. Implementation requires taking initiative. In my personal experience, I've found that a lot of times I receive credit for an innovative idea simply because I took the initiative to act on my idea – in other words, I implemented! When I was looking for a great travel itinerary template for my executives years ago, I kept coming up short. I took that as an opportunity and created one that still gets rave reviews from executives and admins alike. My executive did not ask me to create one, I just did it and came away looking smart. When you exercise initiative and implement your innovative ideas, you'll stand out and look smart, too!

PLAN OF ACTION:

☐ Find a copy of the book *1001 Ways To Take Initiative At Work* by Bob Nelson.

    ○ Read the book.

    ○ Identify areas where you can begin to take more initiative at work.

☐ Identify how you typically approach taking initiative using Stephen Covey's seven levels of initiative. Think about what you can do to advance yourself further up the initiative ladder.

☐ Begin taking more initiative!

☐ Keep a log in your journal or Innovation Binder of when and how you took initiative and the outcomes of each occurrence. Then evaluate how you did and what you'll change or do the same the next time. Keep taking those baby steps forward as you become more comfortable exercising initiative!

CHAPTER 17

SEEK CHALLENGES
THAT STRETCH
YOU

*"One's mind, once stretched by a new idea, never regains its
original dimensions."*

~ Oliver Wendell Holmes

Have you ever volunteered for a challenging project? Do you view the problems that arise in your life as learning opportunities? No one wants more problems or challenges in their lives, but challenges and problems are tools that help us learn and grow.

If we can learn to view challenges as interesting, acceptable, normal parts of our everyday life, they can become a valuable tool to help us expand our innovation abilities. They can teach us things. They help us dig deeper and uncover root causes. They give us the opportunity to come up with new solutions to recurring problems. As we try some of the solutions we devise, we'll find some solutions work better than others. We then apply this new understanding to the next challenge, problem, or opportunity we face. This is how the momentum builds and your creative thoughts suddenly turn into innovative ideas that bear results.

You have to continually visit new places, try new things, seek new information, and experiment to learn new things. So how do you seek new challenges? Start by observing the opportunities that may already be surrounding you. Are there projects at the office that you'd like to participate in but haven't specifically been asked to support? Are there annual charity events that your company sponsors that you could volunteer to get involved with? Are there professional certifications such as becoming a Microsoft Office Specialist that you could pursue? If you belong to professional associations, have you considered becoming a committee member, chair, or running for a board position? Every one of these examples will challenge you and stretch you in new ways. They will present opportunities to learn new things, exercise initiative, brainstorm through solutions to problems, and so much more. What you learn from these experiences will stretch your thinking, help you develop new skills, strengthen your leadership abilities, and give you additional exposure to people and resources that will likely provide additional support in your career development.

One of the best examples of this in my own career is my membership in the International Association of Administrative Professionals (IAAP). When I initially got involved, it was simply to have a professional association listed on my résumé. But then I started attending monthly chapter meetings and got involved in my local chapter's program committee. Over several years of chapter membership and leading the program committee for much of that time, I began to see opportunities for our chapter to create an annual event during Administrative Professionals Week that could potentially fund our chapter's annual budget for the entire year.

In order to make this happen, I had to volunteer a lot more of my time and energy to this cause. I had to immerse myself in learning how to successfully run an event sponsorship campaign. I had to learn how to coordinate and solicit exhibitors for a business showcase, create and distribute a speaker request for proposal (RFP), and effectively market and promote the event to companies and individuals we were trying to reach. It also meant I had to be willing to take on the leadership role of the committee, acting as one of the driving forces behind this initiative. It was an extensive and time-consuming undertaking, but the results were worth it!

Not only did our chapter create an event that could substantially fund our annual budget during my involvement, but I stretched my skills and experience in amazing ways and built some incredible business relationships. These are relationships and skills that I have been able to integrate into what I do every day at the office for my clients and their projects. I didn't know that one day one of my clients was going to begin holding public workshops. But when they did, I was fully prepared to assist them because I had sought out a challenge that stretched me within my IAAP chapter membership. At another time, a client needed to find a graphic designer and wanted to use an RFP process to accomplish this. I was able to quickly modify my speaker RFP and help my client find the designer they needed quickly. The list of how I have used the skills I learned throughout that single event planning experience is endless. The time I invested and the difficulties I faced by seeking this challenge have made me a better administrative resource and problem solver.

"It's simple...go the extra mile and you will stand out from the crowd."

~ Robin Crow

Seeking challenges keeps you fresh, it keeps your thinking fresh, and it prepares you for career opportunities you might never imagine. But sometimes you have to ask for them. So look around you and figure out where you can pursue some new challenges to positively stretch you into a more innovative person!

PLAN OF ACTION:

☐ Think about opportunities that may already be surrounding you.

- ○ Are there projects at the office that you'd like to participate in but haven't specifically been asked to support?

- ○ Are there annual charity events that your company sponsors that you could volunteer to get involved with?

- ○ Are there professional certifications such as becoming a Microsoft Office Specialist (MOS) or a Certified Administrative Professional (CAP) that you could pursue?

- ○ If you belong to professional associations, have you considered becoming a committee member, committee chair, or even running for a board position?

- ○ What are some of the community or professional organizations in your area?

☐ Find out how you can become more involved in one of those opportunities you identify.

- ○ Ask your executive during your next one-on-one meeting or during your annual performance review.

○ Research professional certifications you want to pursue and determine what's involved in achieving them.

○ Ask the organizations you belong to where they need more support or express your specific interests in how you'd like to get more involved with them.

☐ Let the stretching begin...take action and get involved.

☐ Keep track of the challenges you face, the things you learn, and the contacts you make throughout the experience in your journal or Innovation Binder.

PART 4: CONCLUSION

"We have enough historians; we need some pioneers."
~ Ron Jaworski

CHAPTER 18

INNOVATION—THE
KEY TO YOUR
CAREER FUTURE

"Just as energy is the basis of life itself, and ideas the source of innovation, so is innovation the vital spark of all human change, improvement and progress."

~ Ted Levitt

To become *The Innovative Admin*, you must increase your capacity for innovation. Innovation is not a one-time destination, it's an ongoing process throughout your life of generating ideas, testing them, and implementing the best of the best. As an innovator, you will repeat this process over and over and over again. When you embrace the innovation process and understand the ups and downs associated with each stage of innovation, it becomes a much more familiar and enjoyable journey.

Becoming *The Innovative Admin* requires continually stretching yourself, expanding your thinking, exposing yourself to innovative people, opening your mind to new information and ideas, and taking action to modify and adapt those ideas to the situations that come up for you. As you apply these ideas to the situations and experiences in your own life, you will transition from doing things the way they've always been done to taking the initiative to implement better ideas. The more you implement and test your new ideas for improving things one by one, the more insights you gain and the more confident you become in implementing and testing other ideas. You can act with confidence because you've populated your mental database with countless ideas and examples, and you've surrounded yourself with innovative advisors who can support you through the process. You shift from an admin who simply runs in maintenance mode into a leader working towards advancement and change in your company and your profession. The more you do it, the less it scares you. The more you do it, the better you get at navigating the innovation process. The more you do it, the more you stand out as a leader in your field. The more you do it, the more you become *The Innovative Admin*.

Why Innovation Matters

As an administrative professional, you must be innovative if you want to:

1. Advance your career and stay ahead no matter what technological advances, personal transitions, or professional opportunities present themselves.

2. Be successful, poised, and prepared for each opportunity that may come your way.

3. Continue advancing the administrative profession as a recognized, valued, and integral role in the 21st century office.

When you develop and establish the habits I've outlined throughout this book, they become part of your normal routine. They aren't something you even have to think about – you'll find yourself automatically doing them. The natural side effect of establishing these habits is you begin leading yourself in a more focused and proactive way. When you lead yourself forward, others notice. They want to figure out how to do what you're doing. This provides you the opportunity to mentor, coach, and lead others as well. The more you lead others, the more you realize how much you need to keep stoking the innovation fire within yourself. The new habits you've established will support you over and over and over again in this endeavor.

When an Idea Doesn't Work

What happens if you give one of your new ideas a try and it's a total flop? The first thing you must realize is that failure is *not* falling short of your goals. Failure is never even trying to reach them. Some of the things you try are not going to work. Others will. This is part of the innovation process. The key is not to dismiss an idea too early. It may just need additional time or tweaking to make it work the way you intended it to.

When you realize something isn't working the way you want it to, don't call that failure. Call it an opportunity to improve an idea that is still under development. Assess what didn't work about it and why. Does it simply need a small adjustment here or there to make it work as anticipated? Does it need additional components? Ask others to take a look at it and help you identify what you might adjust to make it work better. Hold your own post-event review with your personal advisory board to explore how the idea can be improved.

Thomas Edison didn't invent a working incandescent electric light bulb on his very first try. In fact, it took five separate inventions combined together before his innovation came to life![16] The innovation process takes some perseverance at times. The bigger your idea is, the more time, energy, testing, tweaking, and perseverance it will likely take. You simply have to acknowledge and accept this when you begin and have the confidence in yourself to keep pushing forward.

> *"Inaction breeds doubt and fear. Action breeds confidence and courage. If you want to conquer fear, do not sit home and think about it. Go out and get busy."*
>
> ~ Dale Carnegie

Overcoming Fear and Self-Doubt

There are always going to be moments of fear and self-doubt that you have to overcome. It's natural for every human being. If you're not a risk taker, it can be a nerve-wracking experience to implement a new idea when you aren't quite sure how it's all going to turn out. But you will never know until you try. That's why it's vital for you to have faith in yourself. Often, the fears and anxieties we face are more made up and inflated in our heads than they actually are in reality.

John C. Maxwell, author and internationally recognized leadership expert, has written on this topic. I find Mr. Maxwell's tips especially insightful and helpful as I face my own fears in life:

- The only way to deal with fear is to face it and overcome it.

- The fact is that most fear is not based on fact. Much of what we fear is based on a feeling.

- One of our biggest misconceptions is that courage equals a lack of fear. In actuality, the opposite is true. Mark Twain explained, "Courage is resistance to fear, mastery of fear — not absence of fear." By admitting our fear, we can then challenge its accuracy.

- To do anything of value, we have to take risks. And with risk comes fear. If we accept it as the price of progress, then we can take appropriate risks that yield great reward.

- Sometimes the best way to fight fear is to focus on our reason for confronting it. Is there a force driving us that is bigger than the fear? The firefighter runs into the burning building not because he's fearless, but because he has a calling that is more important than the fear.

- The more we face our fears, the more capable we begin to feel, and the more fears we are willing to face.[17]

As I've applied Mr. Maxwell's concepts to my own experiences, here's some of what I learned that I hope will help you to confront your own fears and give them a swift kick out the door:

- Fear is not all bad. It can be just the push you need to take action.

- Fears only control you when you allow them to. It's a choice.

- No matter who you are or what you know, there are times when you need help and sometimes you have to ASK for it. Then you have to get out of your own way and allow someone to provide the help you need.

- Everyone is human. We all have blind spots. When you surround yourself with the right people, acquire the right skills, gain new perspectives, and pursue new ideas, you set yourself up for unmeasured success.

Different personality types respond to fear differently. Fear stirs up emotions and underlying beliefs we hold whether we realize they existed before or not. But you cannot allow fear to cripple you to the point of inaction. ***Innovators are people of action!*** In his book, *Magnificent Mind At Any Age*, Dr. Daniel Amen explains it like this:

> Facing your fears is a key component of resilience train-
> ing. Allowing fear to take hold and put down roots in
> your brain ensures they will control you later on....
> When you face your fears, you are likely rewiring your
> brain to have control over it. When you hide from your
> fears, they begin to control you. In simple terms it
> means getting back on the bicycle once you have fallen
> off, getting another job after being fired, or becoming
> involved in a new relationship after a messy divorce.[18]

The excitement and relief that comes from overcoming your fears is positively contagious. I highly recommend it! So step out with courage and confidence in yourself and face those fears, doubts, and worries head on. I think you'll find that most of them weren't worth all of the anxiety and concern that you initially invested in them. Turn that energy into action and implement! It's the fast track to success over and over again.

> *"It is arrogant to think that we are perfect and we will
> never fail. We are not programmed with the answers;
> we learn them. We get the right answers by learning
> processes and observing our errors along the way."*
>
> ~ Dr. Daniel Amen

You can do it!

You can become more innovative when you make the conscious decision to do so. The innovation process takes time, patience, and a
positive attitude. But the more you practice the strategies outlined

in this book, the more skilled you'll get at expanding your thinking and the more confident you'll become.

> *"A journey of a thousand miles must begin with a single step."*
>
> ~ Lao Tzu

Remain flexible throughout your journey and don't take yourself too seriously. As one of my mentors reminded me: "Be kind to yourself. You have to remember that what you're doing isn't brain surgery. It's important to you, but it's not the end of the world if things don't go perfectly." We're human, after all, and that means we are going to make mistakes. Just make sure you learn from them.

In this age of advancing technology and evolving business environments, just having good skills and a lot of experience is no longer enough. As individuals and professionals, it's very important to expose ourselves constantly to new ideas, methods, and industry trends if we want to excel. Innovation is a required skill for success. Executives want assistants who can provide solutions to the problems that come up every day. The process of becoming *The Innovative Admin* will make you a better problem solver, collaborator, team member, support person, analytical thinker, and leader. The new ideas and concepts that you learn throughout your journey will find their way into what you do each day on the job. You MUST become an innovator who is constantly adding value if you want to remain a competitive and marketable administrative professional.

If you want to become more than *just* the secretary or administrative assistant…if you want to become an administrative leader in your organization, you MUST learn how to think innovatively and take action. You can remain vibrant and successful if you commit to leading yourself down the path to becoming more innovative. Those admins who become innovators and who get creative about the way they plan their careers will be the ones who thrive in this profession for years to come.

So what are you waiting for? Unleash the power of innovation in your administrative career and become known as *The Innovative Admin*!

APPENDIX

Recommended Reading

If you want to develop a **HEALTHY BRAIN** and expand its creative capacity, read:

- *Magnificent Mind At Any Age* by Daniel G. Amen, M.D.

- *The Creative Brain* by Nancy C. Andreasen

- *Brain Rules* by John Medina

If you want to learn how to change your **MINDSET** and **BELIEFS**, read:

- *Mindset: The New Psychology of Success* by Carol S. Dweck

- *The Belief Quotient* by Dr. Lisa Van Allen *(To be published in Spring 2012)*

If you want to develop a (more) **POSITIVE ATTITUDE**, read:

- *Attitude is Everything* by Jeff Keller

If you want to learn more about **INNOVATION** and how to become more **INNOVATIVE**, read:

- *Innovate Like Edison* by Michael J. Gelb and Sarah Miller Caldicott

- *Thinking Clockwise: A Field Guide for the Innovative Leader* by Dennis Stauffer

- *Stoking Your Innovation Bonfire* by Braden Kelley

If you want to learn how to successfully maneuver any **CHANGE** in your life, read:

- *Change Anything* by Kerry Patterson, Joseph Grenny, David Maxfield, Ron McMillan, and Al Switzler

- *The First 30 Days* by Ariane de Bonvoisin

If you want to learn how to take (more) **INITIATIVE** at work, read:

- *1001 Ways To Take Initiative At Work* by Bob Nelson

If you want to learn more about your **PERSONALITY, STRENGTHS,** and **PASSIONS** read:

- *TypeTalk* by Otto Kroeger and Janet M. Thuesen

- *TypeTalk at Work* by Otto Kroeger with Janet M. Thuesen and Hile Rutledge

- *The Art of Speedreading People* by Paul D. Tieger and Barbara Barron-Tieger

- *StrengthsFinder 2.0* by Tom Rath (includes the assessment)

- *Standout* by Marcus Buckingham (includes the assessment)

- *The New Birth Order Book* by Dr. Kevin Leman

- *Fascinate* by Sally Hogshead

- *The Passion Test: The Effortless Path to Discovering Your Life Purpose* By Janet Attwood and Chris Attwood

Other **RECOMMENDED READING** for *The Innovative Admin*:

- *Crucial Conversations* by Kerry Patterson, Joseph Grenny, Ron McMillan, and Al Switzler

- *Administrative Excellence* by Erin O'Hara Meyer

- *SuperCompetent* by Laura Stack

- *Become An Inner Circle Assistant* by Joan Burge

- *Make a Name For Yourself* by Robin Fisher Roffer

- *Career Distinction* by William Arruda and Kirstin Dixson (includes an assessment)

- *The 7 Habits of Highly Effective People* by Stephen R. Covey

- *The 8th Habit: From Effectiveness to Greatness* by Stephen R. Covey

Develop Healthful Habits for Innovation Success

As I prepared to write this book, I researched several topics related to how our brains actually work and what we can do to increase our learning capacity and our innovative thinking abilities. I knew it was possible to train yourself to think differently. I knew it was possible to create new habits and develop new mindsets. I knew it was important to be living as healthfully as I possibly can. What I didn't understand was how detrimental some of the personal habits we have and the lifestyle choices we make can be to our overall success – personally and professionally.

Dr. Daniel Amen, a clinical neuroscientist, psychiatrist, brain imaging expert, and New York Times best selling author of *Change Your Brain, Change Your Life* gives some insight into the habits in our lives that may be sabotaging our success. In his book *Magnificent Mind at Any Age*, Dr. Amen says, "Your daily habits and routines, as we will see, are either hurting or helping your brain." He then goes on to identify "Fourteen Bad Brain Habits That May Affect All Age Groups:"

1. Lousy diet

2. Lack of exercise

3. Risking brain trauma

4. Chronic stress

5. Negative thinking, chronic worry, or anger

6. Poor sleep

7. Cigarette smoke

8. Excessive caffeine

9. Aspartame and MSG

10. Exposure to environmental toxins

11. Excessive TV

12. Excessive video games

13. Excessive computer or cell phone time

14. More than a little alcohol[19]

That's quite a list! The worst part is some of these habits compound the effects of the others. The longer you ignore them, the harder it becomes to fix them. Your brain is impacted by the daily habits and routines that you choose for yourself. When your brain isn't working at its full potential, you are not able to function as optimally as you need to be either. This ultimately affects your capacity for innovation. You must address these habits if you want to be successful.

For many of us, improved health is a matter of the choices we make. It does take time and effort to achieve and maintain it. In my own life, once I experienced the feeling that comes from eating right, exercising consistently, sleeping well, and removing toxins and stimulants from my diet, all the time and effort I invested to achieve this feeling was completely worth it. And once you achieve it, maintaining it is much easier because you have developed new habits to support the healthy lifestyle going forward. I challenge you to give it a try for yourself.

Asking Your Employer to Support Your Training and Professional Development

I f I walked up to your desk and asked you to give me $20, what would you say? You'd probably respond with, "Why?" or "What do you need it for?" or "I don't have $20, so you need to ask someone else." I can also hear a few smart, sarcastic replies coming my direction…and probably understandably so after all, I didn't even give you any context for my request or what I needed that $20 for.

What if I walked up to your desk and said, "I need $20 from petty cash to pay the pizza delivery guy for pizza at our staff lunch today. Can you help me?" You immediately know a lot more about my reason for making the request. If you maintain the petty cash, you can probably help me. If you don't, you can probably direct me to the right person or the proper procedure for submitting the reimbursement request.

I share these examples because a lot of times when we ask for our employer's support for training or professional development requests, we walk up and ask for their support without providing enough details or a solid business case for why they should consider our request, and many times, their responses are disappointing to us as a result. So what can you do to improve your chances of getting your requests approved for employer support of training and professional development?

Step 1: Do Your Research

Facts are persuasive. Do your homework before you make your request so you know exactly what the training you want will include and what other options may be available in various price ranges, formats (online or teleclass vs. in person), and locations. Have facts and statistics available to support your request. These websites are a great place to find valuable, supporting information and statistics to justify a training investment:

- www.Adminology.org

- www.iaap-hq.org

Step 2: Prepare Your Business Case

You need to think like a business owner or company executive. Build a business case for your training proposal request. Learning what goes into a solid business case is something you'll be able to use throughout your career as you support teams and executives.

The key elements of a good business case include:

- Situational assessment and problem statement

- Request description

- Solution description

- Cost and benefit analysis

- Implementation timeline

- Critical assumptions and risk assessment

- Conclusions and recommendations

When you create your proposal based on relevant information for all of these key areas, you'll be thoroughly prepared for questions or additional information your executive may request from you. I've created **a sample training business case**, which you can **download at www.TheInnovativeAdmin.com**, so you can see what it might look like. It may not always be necessary to submit this much information, but preparing your request by going through this process will ensure you have put the appropriate thought and research into your request BEFORE you make it.

Step 3: Presenting Your Information

Some times are better than others for presenting your request. Avoid rushed, high stress, busy times. Look for opportunities when your executive is in a positive frame of mind and office activities aren't as hectic.

If you know your executive takes in information best when it comes in short, succinct, bulleted lists, then present your business case that way, too. If you know your executive is more relational and likes to know the history and support behind something, then adapt your presentation style to match. Some executives prefer verbal exchanges, some want to see it on paper. I recommend a combination of both. I often suggest planting the seed verbally that you are going to be presenting a training proposal, then water that seed by following up with your written documentation. Your request may require some nurturing, but the effort is worth it when your request is approved.

NEVER make your request in front of a group of your colleagues or co-workers. Your executive may be willing to approve your request because you're a dedicated, hard worker, but that may not be the case for everyone you work with. So don't assume it will be approved for all if it's approved for one.

Always try to present your requests at the beginning of a budget year if you can. Your chances of gaining approval are much better when the funds aren't yet spent or fully allocated. Better yet, submit your request while they are working on budget planning for the year so your request can be built into the budget from the beginning.

If you're smart, you'll also put some thought into how you'll prepare someone else who may need to cover for your absence. Do you have documented procedures for your position? If not, then get started putting your administrative procedures manual together today so you can be out of the office for training and the office is still able to run smoothly in your absence. Visit www.AllThings-Admin.com for free templates to help you get started.

Step 4: Show Return on Investment (ROI)

When you can demonstrate the return on investment (ROI) your company will receive as a result of investing in your training and professional development, the chances of receiving a request approval will also increase. In order to do this, you need to create pre-training objectives you want to achieve. Document new ideas, key takeaways, new relationships you want to build, and the next steps you want to pull from the training.

Document the objective outcomes after the training is completed and share this information with your executive. The IAAP website has a fantastic Return On Investment Planner which you can typically find on their events pages (www.iaap-hq.org).

Step 5: Responding to your training request APPROVAL!

When your request is approved, THANK your executive both verbally and in writing. Send them an email, write them a thank you card, show your appreciation for their support!

Thank them with continued great performance also! Regularly point out the little things you learned that you just used or implemented from the training and how the company or your executive benefitted – continually reinforce the ROI.

What to Do When You Don't Get the Response You Wanted

- Respectfully listen to the reasons for the "No"

- Ask again in a different way or at a different time

- Ask how you CAN help make it possible (brainstorm possibilities)

- Ask what is possible if this is not

- Ask when it may be possible, if not now

- Ask what you can do to improve the way you're asking

- Don't give up! It may be "No – not right now," and NOT a "No – never."

"You don't get what you don't ask for."

~ Julie Perrine

"What you don't ask for stays the same."

~ Unknown

As the technology landscape and the administrative profession continue to change at rapid speeds, it's more important than ever for administrative professionals to stay current in their own professional development. Ultimately, your professional development is YOUR responsibility, not your employer's. But it doesn't hurt to seek their support when they are also a direct beneficiary of the skills and abilities you bring to the position every day. When you assemble a complete, well-researched, solid business case to support your training request, I'm certain you'll find more favorable responses to future requests.

Additional Resources:

- BOOK: *Love It Don't Leave It: 26 Ways to Get What You Want at Work* by Beverly Kaye and Sharon Jordon-Evans

Other Products From All Things Admin

Administrative Procedures Development Products

- *5 Simple Steps to Creating Your Administrative Procedures Binder* ebook

- Administrative Procedures Toolkit

- "Kick-start Creating Your Administrative Procedures Binder" Online Course

Other Products

- Professional Portfolio Builder

- Templates Packages

- On-Demand Audio Training Courses

Visit **www.AllThingsAdmin.com** for more information on these products and many more.

How To Connect With All Things Admin

Visit our blog! www.AllThingsAdmin.com

Become a FAN of All Things Admin!
www.Facebook.com/AllThingsAdmin

Follow Julie Perrine!
www.Twitter.com/JuliePerrine

Connect with Julie Perrine!
www.Linkedin.com/in/JuliePerrine

For **downloadable resources** mentioned in this book, visit:

www.TheInnovativeAdmin.com

About the Author

Julie Perrine

Certified Administrative Professional – Organizational Management
Myers-Briggs Type Indicator Certified Practitioner

Julie Perrine, CAP-OM, is an administrative expert, trainer, motivational speaker, and author. She is the founder and CEO of All Things Admin, a company dedicated to developing and providing breakthrough products, training, mentoring, and resources for administrative professionals worldwide.

Julie has more than 20 years of experience in the administrative profession spanning several industries and serving in corporate and startup settings. Julie's main mission is to guide, encourage, and connect administrative professionals to the innovative technologies, ideas, resources, and people they need as they work toward achieving their career goals. Her upbeat, straightforward, step-by-step approach to handling the opportunities and challenges facing administrative professionals gives them proactive strategies for developing a plan, creating forward motion, and achieving great results.

Julie has created several innovative tools and programs for administrative professionals including the Administrative Procedures Toolkit, Kick-Start Creating Your Administrative Procedures

Binder Course, Professional Portfolio Builder, and e-Portfolio Builder. She has also published an ebook entitled *5 Simple Steps to Creating Your Administrative Procedures Binder*.

Julie transformed a career as an administrative professional into several successful enterprises and shares her knowledge, expertise, and resources with individuals, corporations, and organizations as an online business model consultant, information product guru, and personality type expert. As a Myers-Briggs Type Indicator certified practitioner, she facilitates understanding and communication among individuals and teams to improve performance, communication, self-awareness, and team cohesion through workshops and individual consulting services.

Julie writes regularly for the *Executive Secretary Magazine* and the All Things Admin blog. Her articles have been published in professional association newsletters nationwide. She has been active in local and international organizations, including the International Association of Administrative Professionals.

For more information on hiring Julie to speak at your upcoming meeting or conference:

Julie Perrine, CAP-OM, MBTI Certified
Founder & CEO, All Things Admin
www.AllThingsAdmin.com/speaking

Acknowledgements

How do I even begin to express my sincere and heartfelt appreciation to each of the people in my life who have supported, encouraged, inspired, and in several cases gently prodded and pushed me throughout this book writing journey? This experience has been unlike any other I've had in my life. It stretched me well beyond my personal and professional comfort zones which has led to some awesome personal discoveries and opened some professional opportunities I would not have imagined before this journey began. But I would NOT have pursued or accomplished this great feat without my team of dedicated supporters. I am most blessed to have this incredibly supportive personal and professional network of friends and colleagues in my life.

So it is with deep gratitude that I express my appreciation to the following for their specific contributions:

- To my best friend, my Chief Encouragement Officer, and the most understanding and patient person throughout this journey – my husband, Todd. There were many times when I'm sure he wondered if I'd ever get this project finished, but instead he gently and lovingly prodded and pushed me forward which was exactly what I needed.

- To my friend and colleague, Kathy Fisher, one of the most innovative admins I have ever worked with. Kathy took administrative support to an entirely new level and had applauding executives far and wide. She not only inspired and taught me how to provide a level of administrative support that exceeded expectations, she was the inspiration behind my writing and finishing this book. Kathy lost her battle with cancer while this book was being written, so it is with honor that I dedicate this book to her memory.

- To the executives and clients I have had the privilege of supporting and learning from throughout my career. Fred and Fran Eiben – my first employers – taught me all about customer service and how to have fun at work. Bill Kubon encouraged me to pursue professional development and lifelong learning. Linn Corbett exposed me to the world of public speaking, training, building a team, and the power of personal branding. Patrice Carroll planted the seeds of entrepreneurship long before I was ready to pursue it. Steve Gray watered those entrepreneurial seeds as they sprouted and grew. Blair Wagner and Jane Balvanz introduced me to countless opportunities for sharing my knowledge and passion for this profession with the world through online training, information products, and books. Each of these executives – and several unnamed – has been vital to my success.

- To my team of virtual assistants and project managers – Amber Miller, Christine Morris, Ruth Pierce, and Penny Sailer – who not only provide valued support and expertise, but keep me on track and moving forward each day. I'd be lost without you.

- To my website developer, Suzanne Bird-Harris, one of the first people I met solely because of social media and dreamed of someday working with who now makes my websites look amazing, too.

- To my copywriters, proofreaders, and editors – Ruth Paarmann, Chrissy Scivicque, Jessica Montanez – for your thoroughness in reviewing and editing my writing.

- To my graphic designer, Amy Belice, for her outstanding design work and the continued education she provides me on what good designs should include.

- To my friends and fellow innovative admins – Cindy Pfennig, Kemetia Foley, Karen Seltrecht – who have brainstormed with me, helped with research, proofed manuscripts, and shared personal experiences to inspire the content of this book.

- To my fellow entrepreneurs and business colleagues – Dr. Lisa Van Allen, Barb Gordon, Becky Esker – who have provided valued expertise, coaching, and friendship throughout this journey.

- To Dr. Susan Fenner at the International Association of Administrative Professionals (IAAP) and my fellow IAAP members who encouraged me to finish this book. They continue to motivate me to provide training and resources for administrative professionals worldwide.

- To ALL of the All Things Admin friends, fans, and followers who inspire me to keep creating materials and training that drives and supports them each day - because of you, I get to do what I love to do every day! Thank you.

INDEX

Notes

Chapter 1

1 "An Evolution of Duties," International Association of Administrative Professionals, accessed March 1, 2012, http://iaap-hq.org/ResearchTrends/Administrative_Professionals_Evolution_of_Duties.htm.

Chapter 2

2 Dennis Stauffer, "The four greatest ways we stop ourselves...in business and in life." (Special report from http://www.insight-fusion.com/SpecialReport.asp accessed June 6, 2011).

3 "The Relationship Between Creativity and Innovation," Smartstorming.com, accessed March 1, 2012, http://www.smartstorming.com/articles/the-relationship-between-creativity-and-innovation.

4 "How To Be An Innovative, Not Just Business, Leader" by David Magellan Horth, *Forbes.com Blog,* January 27, 2010. http://www.forbes.com/2010/01/27/innovation-change-strategy-leadership-managing-ccl.html.

Chapter 4

5 Carol S. Dweck, Ph.D., *Mindset: The New Psychology of Success* (New York: Ballentine Books, 2006), 6-7.

Chapter 5

6 "Creating An Innovation Mindset" by Mike Docherty. *Innovation.net Blog*, July 28, 2004, http://venture2.typepad.com/innovationnet/2004/07/creating_an_inn.html.

Chapter 7

7 Braden Kelley, *Stoking Your Innovation Bonfire* (New Jersey: John Wiley & Sons, 2010) 121.

Chapter 8

8 People with the Individualization strength are fascinated with the unique qualities of each person. They have an aptitude for figuring out how different people can work together effectively. See *Strengths Finder 2.0* for more details on the various strengths and information on how to take the Strengths assessment.

9 Daniel G. Amen, M.D., *Magnificent Mind at Any Age* (New York: Three Rivers Press, 2008) 123-124.

Chapter 11

10 "How to Keep a Brain Sharp While Enjoying a Favorite Hobby", accessed March 1, 2012, http://www.ehow.com/how_4614807_brain-sharp-enjoying-favorite-hobby.html.

11 Ibid.

Chapter 12

12 "Business Acumen", accessed March 1, 2012, http://en.wikipedia.org/wiki/Business_acumen.

13 Dan Kennedy, *No B.S. Time Management for Entrepreneurs, No Holds Barred, Kick Butt, Take No Prisoners, Guide to Time, Productivity, and Sanity* (Canada: Entrepreneur Press, 2004) 92-93.

14 Ibid., 97-98.

Chapter 16

15 Stephen R. Covey, *The 8th Habit, From Effectiveness to Greatness* (New York: Free Press, 2004) 133.

Chapter 17

16 Michael J. Gelb and Sarah Miller Caldicott, *Innovative Like Edison: The Success System of America's Greatest Inventor* (New York: Dutton, 2007) 4-5.

17 "What Are Your Fears Keeping You From Doing" by John C Maxwell, *JohnMaxwellOnLeadership.com Blog,* January 10, 2011, http://johnmaxwellonleadership.com/2011/01/10/what-are-your-fears-keeping-you-from-doing/.

18 Daniel G. Amen, M.D., *Magnificent Mind at Any Age* (New York: Three Rivers Press, 2008) 214.

Appendix

19 Ibid., 25-27.